LIBERATING
THE
FUTURE

God,
Mammon,
and Theology

Edited by
JOERG RIEGER

230

Fortress Press   **Minneapolis**

In memory of
Frederick Herzo

LIBERATING THE FUTURE
God, Mammon, and Theology

Cover design by Brad Norr

Library of Congress Cataloguing-in-Publication data

Liberating the future : God, Mammon, and theology / edited by Joerg Rieger.
    p.   cm.
    Includes bibliographical references (p.) .
    ISBN 0-8006-3143-9 (alk. paper)
    1. Liberation theology--Congresses.   2. International economic relations--Congresses. 3. Economic development--Religious aspects--Christianity--Congresses. I. Rieger , Joerg.
    BT83.57.L46 1998   98-44456
    230 ' . 0464--dc21   CIP

Manufactured in the U.S.A.   AF 1-3143
02 01 00 99 98 1 2 3 4 5 6 7 8 9 10

Contents

Preface

This volume explores the frontiers of theological reflection in the radically altered contemporary context. It grows out of a special topics forum at the American Academy of Religion in New Orleans in 1996 on liberation theology at the turn of the century, organized in memory of Frederick Herzog, who had died a year earlier. The importance of the topic and the great deal of attention that the event received, being one of the best attended major events at the annual meeting, prompted us to revise and expand our contributions for publication.

The volume is dedicated to the memory of a theologian who developed one of the initial strands of liberation theology. Teaching and writing as a white male theologian in the South of the United States, the late Frederick Herzog seems a most unlikely participant in the liberation theology project. Yet Herzog, professor of systematic theology at Duke University for thirty-five years, educated in the centers of theology in Bonn, Basel, and Princeton, proved that even mainline theologians can learn how to listen to the voices of the oppressed. His work witnesses to the fact that liberation theology, far from being some kind of special-interest theology, is relevant to all of theology. Herzog's accomplishment raises the hope that more theologians and members of the privileged classes will come to understand the power of God's liberation.

Herzog's story is instructive. He did not develop liberation theology primarily as a response to other like-minded theologies or theologians. His theology took shape in encounters of God's presence in unexpected places, in personal encounters with those who did not matter to theology or the church, like sharecroppers in the fields of North Carolina, African Americans, the poor. For Herzog, all these people had names and stories. Familiar theological worlds were transformed not first of all in theological debates but in personal encounters with those at the underside of history. In all of this Herzog was led to a reconstruction of theology which took shape in mutual accountability to two poles: the divine Other and the human other. In his last book, *God-Walk*, he puts it this way: "Liberation theology begins as the poor begin to listen to each other before God. Liberation theology continues as we listen to the poor before God."[1]

Still under the sway of the shooting of Martin Luther King, Jr., Herzog in 1970 published the first essay on liberation theology to appear in English. He soon found that others had picked up the same theme. The works of James H. Cone, Gustavo Gutiérrez, and Rosemary Radford Ruether were in the making at the same time.[2] In the succeeding years, Herzog became one of the bridge-builders in the North American context and across the Atlantic, forging connections and alliances without disregarding vital differences. His work, sparked by the encounter with the suffering of African Americans in the South,[3] later was further developed in relation to the plight of Latin Americans, women, and more recently Native Americans as well. Herzog pulled together various strands of liberation theology not in order to imitate or supersede them but in order to reform theology and the church, starting at home. In this volume his spirit has brought together the representatives of, and witnesses to, various strands of liberation theology once more.

In the United States, Herzog was a forerunner in understanding the economic underpinnings of various forms of oppression, one of the common threads of the chapters in this volume. While early on he already realized that oppression is not produced simply by political structures or racial prejudices but also by economic structures, his close relationship to Latin America and especially Peru from the late 1980s further contributed to his understanding.

This volume, written by some of Herzog's colleagues and friends who have shared in the struggle for liberation, presents a cross-section of theologians from various countries and diverse academic settings. The work invites theologians and religious persons everywhere to join us in reflection on God's ongoing work of liberation in the midst of suffering and oppression.

Contributors

JOHN B. COBB JR. is Ingraham Professor of Theology Emeritus, Claremont School of Theology, California. Among his most recent books are *Sustaining the Common Good: A Christian Perspective on the Global Economy* (1994) and *Reclaiming the Church* (1997)

GUSTAVO GUTIÉRREZ has often been called the father of liberation theology. He directs the Instituto Barolomé de Las Casas in Lima, Peru, teaches at the Universidad Catolica in Lima, and serves as a parish priest. His recent publications in English include *Las Casas: In Search of the Poor of Jesus Christ* (1993) and *Sharing the Word through the Liturgical Year* (1997). A collection of his writings has recently been edited by James B. Nickoloff, *Gustavo Gutiérrez: Essential Writings* (1996).

FREDERICK HERZOG was Professor of Systematic Theology at Duke University. He is the author of a number of books, including *Justice Church: The New Function of the Church in North American Christianity* (1980) and *God-Walk: Liberation Shaping Dogmatics* (1988).

M. DOUGLAS MEEKS is Cal Turner Professor of Wesley Studies and Theology at Vanderbilt University. Among his books is *God the Economist: The Doctrine of God and Political Economy* (1989). He is also editor of *The Portion of the Poor: Good News to the Poor in the Wesleyan Tradition* (1995).

JÜRGEN MOLTMANN is Professor of Systematic Theology Emeritus at the University of Tübingen, Germany. A prolific author, Moltmann's most recent books in English include *The Source of Life: The Holy Spirit and the Theology of Life* (1997) and *The Coming of God: Christian Eschatology* (1996).

JOERG RIEGER is Assistant Professor of Systematic Theology, Perkins School of Theology at Southern Methodist University. He is author of *Remember the Poor: The Challenge to Theology in the Twenty-First Century* (1998). He is editor of *Theology from the Belly of the Whale: A Frederick Herzog Reader*, forthcoming.

SUSAN BROOKS THISTLETHWAITE is President of Chicago Theological Seminary. Among her recent publications are *Casting Stones: Prostitution and Liberation in Asia and the United States* (1996) and *Lift Every Voice: Constructing Christian Theologies from the Underside* (1998).

GAYRAUD S. WILMORE is Professor of Church History Emeritus, Interdenominational Theological Center (retired). His publications include *Black Religion and Black Radicalism: An Interpretation of the Religious History of Afro-American People* (1983) and *Black Theology: A Documentary History* (1993).

JOERG RIEGER

1. Introduction
Watch the Money

God and Mammon

Jesus' warning that no one can serve two masters is well known. It is impossible, we are told, to serve God and Mammon (Matt. 6:24). In much of theology today there seems, at first sight, to be little danger of their meeting. We have developed a convenient division of labor according to which theology is assigned the study of God and matters of faith, while such "hard" sciences as economics take it upon themselves to watch Mammon. At a time when the market economy is expanding its reach all around the globe, a growing number of specialists are assigned this task. Wall Street may be one of the most important hubs, but there are also the World Bank and a growing number of transnational corporations, supported on the ground by vast armies of accountants and business people.

In recent history theologians, with few exceptions, have not been among the money watchers.[1] Imagine therefore our amazement when all the panelists at a forum on liberation theology at the turn of the century, organized in memory of the late Frederick Herzog, in their own ways had something to say about how economic issues and tensions matter to theology. Gustavo Gutiérrez laid the foundation. He reminded us that already Jesus knew how to watch the money.[2] In the story of the poor widow's offering (Mark 12:41-44), Jesus chooses a specific location at one of the doors of the temple in order to watch people put money into the treasury. Only from this perspective is it possi-

ble to understand the difference between the widow and the
rich man. What if theologians located themselves for instance at
the doors of the World Bank? Whom would we meet? What
would we see? A look into the board rooms and executive suites
of corporate America can also teach us some valuable lessons
about other issues, such as race relations, as Gayraud Wilmore
in his chapter reminds us. The marginalization of women and
children all over the globe (Thistlethwaite), another look at the
doctrines of "economism" (Cobb), a confrontation of the logic of
the market and the logic of faith (Meeks), the challenges of globalization for the First World[3] (Moltmann), the question where
the poor will sleep in the twenty-first century (Gutiérrez), and
the search for a common-interest theology that starts at the
underside of history (Rieger), are all tied together in a growing
awareness of economic injustices.[4]

In the midst of the theological crises of the present, the future
of theology as a whole may well depend on learning what to
watch and how to watch. But if the concept of theology clearly
demands that we focus on God, does not a peek at the economy
merely add distractions? Are liberation theologians now trying to
"economize" the gospel, just as some accused them earlier of
politicizing it? It is time to clear up a whole set of misunderstandings connected to the modern idea of a division of labor
that locates theology outside of political and economic structures.
It is often overlooked that the recent theological focus on politics
was not aimed so much at politicizing theology as at giving an
account of how much modern theology had been politicized
already.[5] The same is true when theology starts to pay attention
to economics. The problem in the global market economy is not
that anything needs to be subjected to the market even more
than it already is but that we need to realize how everything is
already subject to market forces, even theology and our images
of God.

The Signs of the Times

Merely watching the movements of Mammon on its own terms,
however, is not enough. While modern theology has generated a
new openness to the "signs of the times," to use the famous expression which permeated the Second Vatican Council, we are more
than ever in need of a perspective which pays attention to the

underside, the dark side, of those signs as well. Here lies one of the major differences between liberal and liberation theologies.

Our dilemma is that at present, with capitalism celebrating one victory after another, it is becoming even harder to distinguish between God and Mammon. Current trends in society certainly do not encourage us to make this distinction. Wall Street seems to have a message, too; and it often receives more attention than the message preached in the pulpits on Sunday mornings.[6]

Living in relationship with those who have not benefited from the victory of capitalism can teach us much about the radical distinction of God and Mammon. If we want to understand where Mammon encroaches on the position of God, we need to learn how to watch for the features of Mammon that have been hidden from view. In other words, we need to develop a sense for those aspects of the modern economy that people (and perhaps even the specialists) are often not aware of, or prefer not to see. A look at the underside of Mammon's shiny surface is inevitable if we want to understand the false god.

In light of the vast dimensions of economic globalization and its effects, theologians need to develop a new vision. Attempts merely to curb the excesses of modern economy without gaining a deeper understanding of its structures will not help us. Given the omnipresence of Mammon in today's world (and its omnipotence and omniscience), we need to see as clearly as possible who God is. Consequently, instead of acting as liberator, theology needs to help us understand first of all that we cannot liberate the world simply by trying a little bit harder. We need to become aware of the deeper roots of the problem.

In this context, the future of theology in general will be based on an honest account of the actual crises of today's world, an honest account of the limits and responsibilities of theology, and an account of the power of God at work with those suffer the most. What is currently helping us to deepen not only the awareness of crisis but also the awareness of what God can do, is the encounter with those who are most affected by the transformations of today's world. Encountering both the suffering and the hope of Third World workers and peasants, African Americans, women and children, and the poor everywhere, we are still in the process of discovering the blinders of our theologies, starting to learn what many people at the underside of history have known for quite some time.

We need to learn, for instance, that some of the main lessons taught by Mammon are false. It is not true, for instance, that the top floors of this world offer us the clearest perspective. Those at the underside know full well that no perspective is universal in and of itself. In fact the view from the top is narrower than others since, harboring few doubts about its universality, it is unable to take seriously alternative perspectives. As a Latina theologian has pointed out, women from the dominant culture, for instance, do not have to learn a Latina point of view in order to survive.[7] Yet for those on the top floors, theologians included, the future may well depend on learning how to watch with new eyes. Many of us continue to be struck by the lessons learned at the underside, lessons which continue to teach us much about the dominant system and about ourselves. In this context the Bible, now read on the streets and in the fields, in battered women's shelters and in the barrios, is liberated, too. Discussions of the "hermeneutical privilege" of the poor, therefore, do not grow out of elaborate theories or ideologies but out of eye-opening and life-transforming encounters with the marginalized. Romanticizing or idolizing the oppressed is beside the point.

At a time when the cries of the people get louder, the primary question is not the future of liberation theologies themselves. As Gustavo Gutiérrez argues in his chapter, the primary question is the future of God's liberation. Trying to discern the future of God's liberation, many liberation theologians have turned the classic theodicy question on its head. Their concern is no longer primarily the justification of God to the modern mind (Where does evil come from if there is a God?), but attention to what God is doing (If this is what evil looks like, where does God enter the picture?). Theology as a whole would do well to start with new encounters with the work of God instead of an image of God defined by a fixed set of ideas that, as we are finding out, can as easily be put together on the grounds of the teachings of Mammon today as on the teachings of earlier metaphysics.

Where We Are

A new look at the tension of God and Mammon in light of those who are sacrificed to the economic gods invites us to broaden our understanding of the crises of the modern world, including the dilemma of theology. Instead of narrowly focusing on a few select symptoms, like the much-discussed crisis of interpretation or the sometimes lamented, sometimes celebrated, loss of foundations, we need to take a look at the larger crisis which has now reached global dimensions, involving issues that range from ecology to poverty and hunger, to race and gender. Without having to claim a closed circuit of correlation, it is safe to say that no mode of theological reflection remains untouched by these larger issues.

At first sight, things may of course not look so bad from a North American perspective. In the late nineties the economy has done well and the victory of capitalism seems to have taken care of most other rivals in the race for power and the authority to interpret the state of the world. This situation has inspired a few theologians to herald the end of liberation theologies and other theologies that used to interfere with the mainline perspective.[8]

But things are not quite that simple. In some countries the situation has worsened after the market economy triumphed. In many places, from Germany to Peru, unemployment has increased, not decreased. From the Peruvian perspective, Gustavo Gutiérrez reports that social and economic exclusion is still on the rise. The omnipresence of the global economy is matched by the omnipresence of poverty and, in the experience of the Peruvian poor, poverty often correlates with death. On the other end of the spectrum, the sobering reality of the Third World is now also becoming a reality in the First World, as Jürgen Moltmann points out in his chapter, concluding that this new situation makes Third World liberation theologies all the more relevant in the First World. Rates of poverty and the gap between rich and poor have risen even at home, in the United States. Douglas Meeks notes that no other period in the history of North America has seen such sharply rising inequality, and both he and John Cobb examine some of the mechanisms that underlie this development. In sum, the celebrated "victory" of capitalism is not able to do away with the growing witness of the lives of millions who live in poverty even in this country, including children.

The 1996 United Nations report on human development, quoted by Moltmann and others in this volume, reminds us that 25,000 children die every day from preventable causes throughout the world, almost 9 million every year. Are theologians watching? Lately, the United Methodist bishops have given some attention to this problem. In an initiative on children and poverty they point out that in the United States between 1979 and 1989 child poverty increased by 21 percent while the Gross National Product grew by 25 percent. Susan Thistlethwaite adds that since World War II child poverty has increased by a whopping 43 percent. Today more than 15 million children in the United States live in poverty, and 9 million lack basic health care. Preschool vaccinations lag behind those in some Third World nations.[9]

At present, more and more people are becoming aware that the gap between rich and poor is widening, affecting even people in the First World who have traditionally been middle class. Between 1975 and 1990, the wealthiest 1 percent of the U.S. population increased its share of total assets from 20 percent to 36 percent, while the number of people in the U.S. living below the poverty line continues to rise. The gap between poor and rich countries is widening even more dramatically. In seventy developing countries today's levels of income are less than those reached in the 1960s or the 1970s.[10] The annual reports on the world's wealthiest people, as well as the astronomical salaries of certain CEOs, raise questions. A Dallas journalist recently announced on National Public Radio that she did not yet see the discrepancy of rich and poor last year until the pastor of a wealthy local Episcopal church pointed it out to his congregation. She does now.[11] How many Christians and how many theologians see the discrepancy yet?

Economists now tell us that we have failed to face up to the implications of the victory in the cold war. Not that this shift has gone unnoticed. But we have yet to understand its far-reaching consequences, among them the question of how the victory changes the situation of the victors. According to the authors of *The Judas Economy*, who confess to be "great believers in the dynamism of the free market," the global market no longer benefits the work force of the First World automatically, as it has done ever since the days of Christopher Columbus. Capital is divorcing itself more and more from the work force everywhere.[12] While this experience is not unfamiliar to many people around the globe, the First World now shares in it, too. As Moltmann observes, the globalization of business apparently leads in our societies not to solidarity but to division.

The market now pushes its own theology, preached not only on Wall Street but also in everyday relationships. Some economists, clearer on this issue than many theologians, begin to understand that Mammon is displacing God.[13] People are now looking to the market for answers, not to the insights and values of their religious traditions. Of all the agendas that theology will set itself for the twenty-first century, which ones are taking seriously this challenge? If this theology of the market is not detected, it will continue to sink more and more into our theological unconscious.

Why do we put up with a situation where the world's 358 billionaires are wealthier than the combined annual income of countries with 45 percent of the world's population? A recent article argues that the market has become not only a substitute for religion but a religion in its own right, if religion is defined as that which makes us understand the world and our place in it. After the collapse of communism this market is quickly becoming a true world religion, the "most successful religion of all time, winning more converts more quickly than any previous belief system or value-system in human history."[14] The author, David Loy, is hopeful that traditional religions can provide an alternative, showing that the values and ideals of the market are not inevitable and natural, thus encouraging us to take theology seriously again. But what if our theologies and our churches have, at least unconsciously, become part of the religion of the market? What if the God worshipped on Sunday mornings looks more like Mammon every day? In this context, it is important to learn how and where to watch. We need more than a dialogue about the problematic doctrines and moral deficits of the new religion. Theology must also deal with its own economic underpinnings. In which structures is our theology rooted? Are alternative structures available?

At this point the jump into postmodernity does not automatically help much since postmodernity itself is tied to the logic of late capitalism.[15] Jean Baudrillard, one of those European intellectuals fascinated by the developments in North America and its leadership position in both the modern and postmodern world, detects the conditions of postmodernity already in the United States of the 1980s. Like Gutiérrez, he finds that postmodernity introduces a certain amnesia in which the struggles and faultlines of American history are simply forgotten. In this situation the poor are no longer credible.[16] Baudrillard discerns a state of "enchantment" in American society that has slowly eroded the awareness of those who suffer, together with the awareness of any limits and boundaries. Has theology, for all its use of the new sentiment in tearing down older boundaries and foundations that are no longer helpful, become part of that wider enchantment that forgets those at the margins? Gayraud Wilmore in his chapter reminds us of what those who are now dismantling affirmative action in California and elsewhere often forget, namely that the conditions of postmodernity have not neutralized the particularities of race, color, and ethnicity. But even if those at the underside are not completely forgotten in postmodernity, the basic problem, in my judgment, is that rather than being challenged, the contemporary postmodern mind is entertained by differences in taste and style. This tendency reaches all the way into the theological arena, where notions of otherness and difference are now becoming more and more fashionable.

In my chapter I point out that the insight into the breakdown of the monolithic thought patterns of modernity has emerged in different places, not only in postmodern philosophies but also in the experience of brokenness at the underside of history. While the critique may sound similar, the implications are different: liberation theology is not interested in pluralism for its own sake but maintains a concern for the marginalized and a desire for connecting with other perspectives from the underside of history. Susan Thistlethwaite in her contribution to this volume introduces a helpful distinction between postmodernists who conform to the norms of the global market economy and those who resist.

No doubt, the victory of capitalism affects not only the victims but also the victors. Both have been sucked into that giant vacuum created by the fact that the market economy is slowly displacing other options that used to help us structure our lives. The modern self, author and source of much of modern theology, is now even less in a position than ever to function as a reliable guide through the maze of the new world order. Confronted with massive suffering, theology can no longer afford to continue with business as usual. The need for listening to those who are silenced grows ever stronger. Here lies the future not only for liberation theologies but for theology as a whole. Perhaps the primary failure of theology is that we have not paid close enough attention yet. Here may well lie one of the deepest roots of the current crisis of theology.

Entering a New Era?

Already there are signs of a new era as well. In response to the cry for liberation, which is getting louder all over the globe, new ways of listening are emerging. Editor of a recent book that calls our attention back to the grassroots at home, Susan Thistlethwaite has argued that the next step in North American liberation theology depends on a new relation to the other. The concern for those at the margins is often misunderstood to mean relief efforts. At a time when the volunteer spirit is still high in the United States,[17] we need to realize that liberation is a two-way street. The one-way street models of charity and handouts, practices which even today still define much of the mainline churches' response to suffering, have not yet allowed for genuine encounters with those at the underside of history. In this way, the benefactors and givers safely remain in control.[18]

This attitude has had detrimental consequences for those who were supposed to be on the receiving end. George Tinker, a Native American theologian, tells the "history of good intentions"[19] of the missions to Native Americans. Unable to learn from the other, missionaries tended to idealize their own culture and approached their work with an inadvertent attitude of condescension. This facilitated the exploitation of the Indians, despite the moral integrity of the missionaries and the fact that the missionaries did not benefit from exploitation themselves.[20] Slowly it is becoming clear that the other is not just recipient but is in fact part of the self that tries to reach out. Nevertheless, it is impossible to merely think one's way into the position of the other. Thistlethwaite reminds us: "You have to *go there* and you have to *be there*."[21] New relationships are already being built on these grounds.

In the encounter with the other, a clearer vision of the "Babylonian captivity" of theology and the church emerges. Our captivity to contemporary political and economic powers is brought to light in a special way in collaboration with those who are most affected by those powers and feel the pain they inflict in their own bodies. Ultimately, the transformation of theology and the church depends on bringing together the claim of the divine Other who resists the widely accepted divinity of Mammon, and the claim of the human other. No Other without the other. No wonder some of us are not convinced by the more recent critiques of accommodation in theology that, while critiquing modern foundational-

ism and advocating the otherness of God and even the church, still
do not notice the marginalized other. The future of theology in general will depend on whether we are able to understand that both
the human other and divine Other are calling us to account.[22]

There is evidence that some people in the churches, laity and
clergy, are beginning to understand. The United Methodist bishops have recently put it this way: "The crisis among children
and the impoverished and our theological and historical man-
dates demand more than additional programs or emphases.
Nothing less than the reshaping of the United Methodist Church
in response to the God who is among 'the least of these' is required."[23] The task is to reshape theology and the church in light
of the underside of history. Are the bishops aware of the radical
break that the new era requires? What about theology?

The editors of a recent volume on liberation theology and postmodernity in the Americas point out that "black, womanist, feminist, American Indian, gay, and Latin American liberation theologies made America the land of the second reformation."[24] This
reformation would in fact be the first on American soil since even
North American Protestantism has always been a "Protestantism
without Reformation," to use Dietrich Bonhoeffer's phrase. We
still need to face the full implications of the fact that the United
States, perhaps more than any other country, has absorbed first
modernity and now postmodernity culturally and economically,
with all its promises and shortcomings.[25] In the Americas, liberation theologies have been among the first indigenous critiques
of modern reason and its effects on economic and political structures. Liberation theologies now expose the instability of many of
our commonly accepted categories. That similar processes are
taking place in many different locations is encouraging. Sandra
Harding, a philosopher of science, has noted that "the destabi-
lization of thought" by feminist critiques "often has advanced
understanding more effectively than restabilizations."[26]

While voices critical of modernity have increased exponen-
tially in recent years, nobody could be more aware of the extent
of the current crisis than those who have been more or less
excluded from its benefits all along, like the majority of people of
Third World countries, African Americans, and many women.
There is a growing awareness that the promises of the modern
United States have not worked for many people. Freedom and
opportunity have not been available to all. Despite heavy smoke-

screens, which are often religious in nature, the hidden faultlines of North American society slowly become visible. A recent essay on growing up poor and white in Oklahoma, part of a larger project on the lives of poor white Americans, formulates the challenge of those at the margins: "We are the proof of the lie of the American dream."[27] Having contributed to the formation and expansion of the United States on the frontiers, even vast numbers of whites who were supposed to share in the American dream remained poor. The lives of most African Americans have been even further removed from the American dream. No wonder that the few dissenting voices in the North American churches, already noted by Bonhoeffer in the 1930s, came out of the black churches. Much to his surprise, he found that the gospel of Jesus Christ was most alive in the black churches of Harlem, in the midst of suffering and hope.[28]

Theology is now being reformed by listening to the plight of the people before God, trying to understand where theological reflection so far has failed them. Here a vast field of investigation opens up. At present, no reformation can take place if the twofold conquest of modern history is not addressed, the assimilation and domestication of both God the Other and the human others which, riding the waves of global economic expansion, ultimately extends its reach to the environment and all of creation.

Whether the transformation of Christianity in the United States will catch on remains to be seen. It will look different than the Reformation of the sixteenth century in many ways. This time it probably will not be identified mainly with the names of a few great theologians. It may also take longer to take hold since it emerged first at the underside of history and no princes or government officials are likely to make it an institution. Being in touch with those who suffer everywhere, this transformation will be more global and will include a broader range of issues, including political and economic matters. God's work cannot be limited to the church. Finally, a new reformation will once again lead to a reformulation of the heritage of the church. Liberation theologies understand that, as Frederick Herzog once put it, "the true 'creeds' of today are bled out of the sufferings of the martyrs in the church of the oppressed."[29] At a time when much of the polarization within theology and our churches seems to have become self-serving,[30] our theological future will depend on listening to the many voices at the underside of history, that part of contemporary reality that refuses to go away despite increasing postmodern pluralism and the related political, economic, and theological shifts.

A Global Effort

This volume draws together a set of distinct voices from various parts of the world that build on each other. Susan Brooks Thistlethwaite identifies as the major roadblock for liberation theology in the United States the failure of economic analysis to take hold, a problem which also has its impact on more radical North American theologies, including black theology and white feminist theology. A powerful false consciousness draws even the oppressed into voting against their own economic interests. The only way out of the dilemma, in Thistlethwaite's account, is to return to the grassroots base of liberation theology.

The chapter by John B. Cobb Jr. develops the economic theme further, observing that the world today is organized around the service of Mammon, a phenomenon he calls "economism." New insights into the idolatrous character of economism and more attention to the suffering of those who are left out are designed to help us understand one of the major sins of our own time and to work against the all-pervasive idealization of the global economy.

M. Douglas Meeks encourages all liberation theologies to pay more attention to the fundamental problem of economic injustices. He develops alternatives to the logic of the market, which constantly interrupts the formation of movements for liberation. In thinking about the church as the economy of God, embodying the logic of grace, praise, and sharing, Meeks identifies new centers of resistance that help to overcome the market's logic of scarcity.

Jürgen Moltmann introduces the notion of globalization, which brings the situation of the Third World to the First World. Recalling the origins of liberation theology and political theology, Moltmann determines the goals for a common future, such as the liberation of both oppressors and oppressed and sharper focus on the life that the reign of God brings.

Gayraud S. Wilmore broadens the horizon from the perspective of the African American community. He explains the importance of black theology's concern for black culture in light of the strict divisions in the "world house" between lower and upper classes. Black theology is encouraged to find new ways of using this culture in resisting dominant values, without being seduced by it. Collaboration with others who live in the basement of the world house can only happen where each group takes seriously its own particular situation. Facing the future of a global economy that will be fascinating to some but cruel to others, Gustavo Gutiérrez renews the fundamental contribution of liberation theology, the preferential option for the poor, which is grounded in God's grace. Gutiérrez, who has often been called the "father of liberation theology," reminds us that the main concern is not the future of liberation theology but Christ's liberation of those who suffer.

In my essay I seek to clarify a major misunderstanding of liberation theology that has frequently impeded its impact, especially in North America. Liberation theology is not "special interest theology" but poses a challenge to all of theology since it addresses the common good from new angles, which include a new understanding of context as that which hurts, the addition of new layers to the view from the underside of history, and a connection of the irruption of God and the eruption of the people.

With the article by Frederick Herzog, we are including in this volume the last work of the theologian whose memory brought us all together. Here Herzog takes a deeper look at our current theological blindness and its relation to past history. The death of 100 million Indians from Hispaniola to Wounded Knee and the continuing plight of Native Americans might shock us into a new awareness of God's walk among the suffering and a new freedom from Mammon's demonic powers.

As the chapters show, serious interaction with the underside of the prevailing system intersects in various ways, even though it grows out of such different social locations as the African American community, the feminist struggle, and other struggles for liberation in Europe, North America, and Latin America. The contributors to this volume represent a diverse group that does not, of course, pretend to speak for all of liberation theology. Other important voices that need to be heard on these issues must include womanist, *mujerista*, Native American, Hispanic, Asian American, and other international perspectives. Yet it is hoped that these voices might all be joined in a search for manifestations of God's liberating power today.

SUSAN BROOKS THISTLETHWAITE

2. On Becoming a Traitor
The Academic Liberation Theologian and the Future

I learned to do liberation theology because I was able to experience the profound contextuality of what Paulo Freire means by *conscientization*.[1] Picture an advanced-seminar room with a long table running down the middle of it. I, and the only other two women then in seminary (this is the early 1970s) sit at one end, the few African American men would sit at the other end. The teacher and the white male students would sit in the middle. One of the books we read, I remember, was Gustavo Gutiérrez's *Theology of Liberation*. The students would all yell at each other, and the teacher would write it all down. Then he would go away and type up everything everyone said and the next week hand out what he had typed. He would ask us if we had said it and if we really meant it. That teacher was Frederick Herzog.

I still have all of these papers in my files. This is what liberation is. It is to experience yourself not as an object of theological reflection, but as an agent. You begin to understand yourself as a human being, a serious human being who can act in the world. I learned to take myself seriously as a theologian. Anyone writing down what you say forces you to take yourself darn seriously. And I learned both to stand up for feminist liberation, to answer, when asked, "Did you say it and did you mean it?" "Yes, I said it, and yes, I meant it." In the deepest sense that is what Nelle Morton meant when she talked about hearing someone "into speech."[2] And furthermore, from this method, I learned that any liberation movement is a partial articulation of what we are yearning for in God's coming reign.

Liberation Theology and the Future

Liberation theology as a self-conscious way of doing theology has existed for slightly more than a quarter century. Yet no liberation theologian I know would argue that it was "invented" only that many years ago. Because liberation theology roots itself in reflection on the life of God in the world, its message, I would like to argue, I hope without sounding sententious, is eternal. Because it is about the life of God in the *world*, it reflects on real historical changes and thus is part of history, not a static pronouncement of a once-for-all revelation.

I used the term *liberation movement.* I would argue that one of the most distinguishing features of liberation theology is that it is tied to movements of people throughout the world who have been impoverished, jailed, tortured, beaten, deprived of basic human rights, and treated as nonhumans.

While it was certainly Herzog who taught me the method of liberation theology, the reality of the movement at the base of liberation theology I learned from becoming active in the battered-women's movement. As a local church pastor in Durham, North Carolina, in the early 1970s I helped to start a rape crisis hotline. At that time there were no other services for women in central North Carolina, and women who were battered by their husbands would also call the hotline. They always seemed to say two things, first, "Let me speak to the pastor," and then "I'm a Bible-believing Christian, but. . . ." As the pastor, I got these calls, and I eventually gathered these women together in Bible study groups. In exactly the same way that the Bible funded the rise of critical consciousness in Central and Latin America,[3] these Bible study groups helped the women to come to grips with the fact that God did not sanction this violence against them and that they, created in the image of God, were not destined for bondage but for freedom. This process is not automatic; it comes from connecting the real experience of oppression to a social analysis, which is then applied to prevailing biblical interpretation. One becomes suspicious that the prevailing interpretation of the scriptures favors the powerful, the oppressor in the dominant culture, and that the gospel message is being hidden and distorted. This is the famous "hermeneutic of suspicion" that was first articulated by Juan Luis Segundo.[4]

For women, we must also struggle with the patriarchalism of the original texts, and so there is a double movement of interpretation where the hermeneutical circle does not stop with a recognition of the liberating message of the gospel text, but must, in fact, be turned *against the text itself* so that women can see themselves as full participants in God's intention for human life to be whole, well, and one.[5] In this sense, liberation theology that pays attention to gender issues is not the second act, but the third.

The future of liberation theology depends on its not losing contact with these grassroots movements for social change. Indeed, in North America and in various places around the world, where people's movements have been co-opted into social services (the U.S.) or muted due to rising living standards (Asia), or where a visible, common enemy has become more elusive and difficult to define (South Africa), liberation theology has become disconnected from the grassroots. When this happens, it ceases to exist. A solely academic liberation theology is not liberation theology. Liberation theology must stay connected to its roots in these larger, albeit very imperfect human movements for change. These movements are what Ken Smith, a Vietnam veteran who is now the director of a model shelter and rehabilitation program for homeless veterans, describes as the "interconnection of souls." He says, "That is the commonality of the experience, that thousands, hundreds of thousands, even millions of people were touched by this."[6]

This is the distinguishing characteristic of liberation theology, its deep and abiding root in movements of human beings who are searching, sometimes inchoately but nevertheless with the knowledge that comes directly from the existential pain of the experience of oppression (the so-called epistemological privilege of the oppressed) for greater justice in their lives. It is not that the oppressed "know more" than those who are more privileged, it is *what they know* about oppression because they are directly affected by it. Even the "friends of the poor," those who try to be in solidarity with the poor but who are not poor themselves, never have this clear a view.

The movement location of liberation theology gives rise to what liberation theologians call *praxis*. Praxis means that theological reflection starts in the political, social, and economic realities of people's lives, this movement base, and then uses the tools of the social sciences, primarily economics, political science, and sociology, to analyze that reality. Theological reflection is done in light of this analysis. This is why Gustavo Gutiérrez defines liberation theology as "the critical reflection on praxis in light of the Word of God." Theory and practice are never separated but flow one into the other; the dualism of subject and object is overcome.

The social movement base of liberation theology and its use of these critical tools of the social sciences distinguish it from one of its forebears, liberalism.

Defend Us from Our Friends and Not Just Our Enemies

One of the dangers to the future of liberation theology, and here I speak of the United States in particular, is the tendency for liberals to assume they understand and embrace liberation method, though they are not willing to take the radical leap that liberation theology demands. In this sense Friedrich Schleiermacher was more an enemy of liberation method than Karl Barth because of the role of both individualism and romantic progressivism in Schleiermacher's work.

What liberalism forgets is that God has two natures, both love and justice. Schleiermacher understood the importance of the love of God, but he did not wrestle with the concept of justice. In a chapter on "Schleiermacher and the Problem of Power," Herzog argues that "in spite of all the progressive features of his [Schleiermacher's] thought, the new world view he promotes is also the mainstay of the given social world of his day—and partly an attempt to legitimate it."[7] Herzog notes that it is Schleiermacher's idealism that leads him to promote the "universal love of humanity."[8] Ideals of freedom and equality were divorced, in Herzog's interpretation of Schleiermacher, from the reality of the poor. It is a theology of the middle class, which does not recognize that its freedom depends on the unfreedom of others, that its culture depends on the existence of the uncultured, that its wealth depends on the poverty of others. "In Schleiermacher there is the tension between ideal equality and the overlooked reality of unreconciled conflict."[9]

This has also been a problem in the kind of white feminist theology which has been rooted in both the movement emphasis of liberation theology (battered-women's movement, rape crisis movement, etc.), but which has also inherited the progressive humanism of the Suffrage movement and its middle-class base, as well as Protestant liberalism's appeal to individual experience. This kind of white feminism, therefore, has rarely acknowledged the conflict between women of other races and white women because liberal humanism has no way to understand history as conflictual.

Liberalism in the United States opened theology to experience and to history and is an important forebear of liberation theology. Yet, and here I am describing the U.S. theological scene, the limit of the historical analysis used by Protestant liberals has generally been its use of psychology, especially when these methods have been generated out of theories that are classist, sexist, and racist in their origins.[10]

The psychological paradigm has led many liberals to embrace a therapeutic approach to social change. An excellent example of this would be the hegemony of the twelve-step programs first used by Alcoholics Anonymous. As Linda Mercadante has shown, the spread of this program as a religious paradigm has had a profound cultural impact on how Americans think about their own ills and that of their society. The sin/grace rubric of Christianity has been replaced with the addiction/recovery model as the twelve-step model has been expanded beyond recovery from alcohol addiction. "Especially in the United States, recovery groups have become for many people fillers of a spiritual vacuum or replacements for rejected religious backgrounds."[11] The joke is that everyone not in recovery is in denial. This then becomes the human predicament.

An example of this is the application of the twelve-step program to social issues such as prostitution. I have worked with prostitutes for the last five years as a volunteer through a fine program called Genesis House. This program describes itself as a home of "hospitality" for women who are in prostitution or who are seeking to leave prostitution. Certainly virtually all those involved in prostitution in the United States have substance abuse problems, and twelve-step programs for alcohol and drug abuse have been an important part of their dealing with these addictions. Yet a twelve-step program for prostitution also exists. The notion of addiction to and recovery from substance abuse has now been applied to a broad social and political and economic phenomenon, namely prostitution. (This also brackets the economic and political aspects of alcohol and drug abuse).

In the work Rita Nakashima Brock and I have done on a liberation theology of prostitution in Asia and the United States, we visited many programs that work with prostitutes throughout Asia as well as the U.S. In Korea, workers in "My Sister's Place" could give a very cogent analysis of the role of economics, militarism, Confucianism, and a host of other systemic factors in the rise of prostitution in Korea. In the United States, none of these social forces is seen to have any influence on prostitution. Prostitutes are dealt with as people who are "addicted to sex." This has a profound impact, in my experience, on their individual self-esteem and is a road-block, ironically, to their leaving prostitution. It also means that these excellent programs for prostitutes have virtually no impact on the social, political, and economic conditions that perpetuate prostitution in the U.S.[12]

Sin is perhaps the doctrine on which liberation theology has had the most impact. Identification of social and systemic sin and evil as a reality, in addition to individual sin, has been a profound contribution by liberation theology to world theology. Mary Potter Engel writes:

> Evil and sin together may be called "wickedness," the complex condition of the lack of right relations in the world in which we live naturally, socially and individually. Though they are inseparable, it is important to distinguish the two. Evil, as Latin American liberation theology has taught us, is systemic. It is not superpersonal forces but structures of oppression; patterns larger than individuals and groups with a life of their own that tempt us toward injustice and impiety—social, political, economic arrangements that distort our perceptions or restrain our abilities to such an extent that we find it difficult to choose or do good. By contrast, sin refers to those free, discrete acts of responsible individuals that create or reinforce these structures of oppression. Neither causes the other; evil and sin are mutually reinforcing.[13]

Identification of these "patterns larger than individuals and groups" as the focus of praxis and theological reflection is a critical theological move that distinguishes liberation theology from liberalism.

Economic Analysis

Major roadblocks hamper doing liberation theology in North America, and not the least of them is aptly illustrated by the last elections. Americans were characterized as complacent and satisfied. As a *Chicago Tribune* article on November 8, 1996, rhapsodized, "We live in placid times . . . this is the calmest period since World War II. No six-year span has been as crisis-free as the 1990's." Calm for whom? Crisis-free for whom? Let's look at the most vulnerable in U.S. society since World War II and measure the impact of this calm on them. In the U. S. the most vulnerable are children of all races and they are in crisis.

The gap between rich and poor in the United States is wider than at any time since World War II. The U.S. is twice as affluent as it was in 1964, when child poverty was actually declining. Yet between 1979 and 1989 child poverty increased by 21 percent while the Gross National Product increased by more than one fourth. Since World War II child poverty has actually increased 43 percent. The top 20 percent of American households increased its share of the national income by more than $116 billion between 1967 and 1992. The poorest 20 percent now have only 5 percent of the nation's income. According to the Economic Policy Institute, the upper 10 percent of U.S. families gained as much income in the 1980s, $543 billion, as did the remaining 90 percent. The U.S. now has the highest rate of poverty in more than thirty years. More than 15 million American children live in poverty, 9 million lack basic health care, rates of preschool vaccinations lag behind many developing nations.[14] My colleague at Chicago Theological Seminary, Ted Jennings, is leading the American United Methodist Bishops in a priority on children and poverty, and he has identified these shocking trends as posing a theological crisis. He is right.

Every two hours a child is killed by gunfire in the United States. Between 1967 and 1991, 50,000 American children died from guns. Homicide is now the third leading cause of death of American children. At a conference on children and health sponsored by the Carter Center in 1995, the physicians attending named "children and handguns" as the single most threatening health care issue in the lives of children. Almost 3 million children were reported abused or neglected in 1992, one every 11 seconds.[15]

Furthermore, our electoral process produces a leadership that is characterized by its opponents as liberal, and yet signed a welfare bill that is driving more and more children below the poverty level to the level of destitution. A related issue is the way welfare reform is related to workfare. In New York City, for example, 23,000 full-time employees of the departments of sanitation and parks have been fired and are being replaced with lower paid workfare recipients who receive no benefits and have no grievance rights or protection against unsafe working conditions. Rev. Peter Laarman, pastor of Judson Memorial Church in New York City and the leader of a coalition of 70 churches, synagogues, and nonprofit agencies, said, "They're not even receiving a living wage . . . It's a form of slavery."[16]

A major roadblock to the emergence of liberation theology in the North American context is the failure of economic analysis to take hold. Though the causes are too numerous to name fully in this chapter, the failure of economic analysis affects even those North American theologies deemed more radical.

Black theology does not root itself in economic analysis. The work of James H. Cone, which does employ a liberation method and economic analysis, is described as being "out of touch with the black churches" by other black theologians. Womanist theologians, such as Delores Williams, are beginning to raise questions about the economic roots of the African American context in North America, as she does in *Sisters in the Wilderness*, but this is still a nascent movement. White feminism has failed almost completely to analyze economics, with the notable exceptions of Beverly W. Harrison, Carter Heyward, Rosemary Radford Ruether and a very few others—powerful folks, to be sure, but whose work is not often appropriated at the grassroots level.

Tools of radical economic critique are not innocent in this failure. Despite the critical move that Karl Marx makes to stand G. W. F. Hegel on his head and to show that liberation is a historical rather than a mental act,[17] the meaning of liberation gets distorted by Marx's views. Marx's description of unalienated, nonexploitative labor illustrates this. "In my *production* I would have objectified my *individuality, its specific character*, and therefore enjoyed not only an individual *manifestation of my life* during the activity, but also when looking at the object I would have the individual pleasure of knowing my personality to be *objective, visible to the senses,* and hence a power *beyond all doubt.*"[18] Privileging work and productivity as the defining moments of humanity and the basis for his analysis lead Marx to neglect most of women's activities (childbearing, child rearing, care of the home, etc.) in favor of more public (i.e. more male oriented) understanding of work. His emphasis on individuality and objectivity neglects values of relationality and community. Further, his critique of capitalism and its political economic relations cannot account for the multiple roles that race plays in economic activity. Race is a major motor of capitalist manipulations of the labor force, but race prejudice will also persist even when it is counter-productive, that is, when it is not productive of capital. A ready example of this would be the tenacious attachment to slavery in the nineteenth century U.S., even after it was less economically viable. Racism needs an economic analysis, because economic exclusions are often the form racism takes, but racism is not fully explained by economic analysis.

Nevertheless, these reservations apply to social critics and are not an explanation of the failure of economic debate to emerge in the United States. For that we have to look to a pervasive ideology of complacency about America's economic prowess. Eroding this complacency and introducing the notion of economic analysis is hard-going. The media supply this complacency with literally thousands of images that support the stereotype. Take, for example, the large number of popular situation comedies featuring middle-class or even upper-class African Americans on television today. This drenches the American psyche with the notion that actual African Americans are moving into the "American dream," and not further into Malcolm X's nightmare. And then white middle-class America is stunned with the O.J. Simpson acquittal.

Backlash against affirmative action seeks to pit white women against African Americans with the stereotype that white women have been integrated into the workforce. This does not appear to be the case in the American military, who have been using, as has the business sector, sexual harassment to send the clear message to women: you do not belong here. And once again, women of color are caught between analyses. The gap between perception and reality, when it is starkly revealed, shakes the nation to the core and then is quickly covered up.

This is the mountain of complacency that a liberation analysis faces if it is to take hold even in poor communities in the United States.

A powerful false consciousness in the United States draws even the oppressed into voting against their own economic interests, and it is to this false consciousness that we must direct our attention, even while we do more complex gendered and raced economic analyses. Unless you do your economic homework, you can't pretend to be doing liberation theology. I feel like screaming this sometimes to my students who tell me they'd like to "add a little liberation theology" to their senior theology papers. To this I reply, "Liberation theology is not a side order of fries. Unless you're willing to take this method all the way, don't even bother with it."

Postmodernism

A final challenge to the future of Liberation theology that I want to name is postmodernism. In the last decade or so, a host of theories has emerged to critique the claims of objectivity and reason of Western scholarship. The so-called postmodernists take their name from their initial diagnosis that the ideal of objectivity and rationality, so beloved of the Western academy, is indeed a culturally produced phenomenon, situated in the context of modernity, and that modernity is on the decline. The postmodernist critique is wide-ranging, linking such diverse concepts as the self, subjectivity, history, art, and architecture, to name only a few.

While the notion that ideas themselves are socially and culturally located is not new, the postmodernist critique has gone much farther, calling into question the verifiability of any distinctions between truth and falsity, good and bad, fact and superstition since these are all concepts that belong to modernity and they cannot be legitimated outside its now-dubious norms.

The modern is almost equated in postmodernism with transcendent reason and its myth that reason could be separated from the body and from history and social location. Because of this, postmodernism has at first appeared attractive to feminists who see its identification of the autonomous reason as a cultural product as similar to the feminist critiques of a masculinist, abstract reason that denigrates women and the earth as symbolic of the body and materiality. While it has had less appeal to liberation theologians, since many of these theologians do their work outside the West, some have found postmodernism's critique of the self as autonomous individual to be congenial. The theorist of prostitution that Rita Brock and I use in our book *Casting Stones*, Thanh-dam Truong, a Vietnamese woman, uses philosopher Michel Foucault.[19] In our liberation theology of prostitution, we use Truong extensively in order to correct trends in liberal feminism's treatment of prostitution as essentially one transhistorical, global phenomenon when it takes on dramatically different meanings over the centuries and in different parts of the world and is, indeed, not one unitary phenomenon in even one country.

Yet many would argue that postmodernism calls into question the possibility of any feminist theology or any liberation theology, because finally these perspectives depend on some kind of unitary concept such as "women" or "the poor." In turn, feminist and liberation theologians question a postmodern intellectualism that begins to question the concept of self and agency just as millions of people around the world are beginning to cry out for selfhood and historical agency. Christine Di Stefano notes that "Nancy Hartsock has asked, Why is it, just at the moment in Western history when previously silenced populations have begun to speak for themselves and on behalf of their subjectivities, that the concept of the subject and the possibility of discovering/creating a liberating 'truth' become suspect?"[20]

I have found Hartsock herself helpful in determining how to use postmodernism without letting it use me. Hartsock notes the usefulness of Albert Memmi's work *The Colonizer and the Colonized* for understanding the situation of postmodernism vis-à-vis feminism and for understanding the postmodernists themselves. Memmi argues that it was necessary for the colonizer to create the category of devalued "other" as a precondition to "the creation of the transcendental rational subject outside of time and space, the subject who is the speaker in Enlightenment philosophy."[21] The resemblance of the colonized to women is remarkable, as every dependent, backward, irrational trait is projected onto the colonized, while the colonizer is the rational subject.

It is this colonizer self who is rightly the object of the postmodernist critique: the colonizer voice is the voice of theory. But, "decolonization struggles, movements of young people, women's movements, racial liberation movements—all these represent the diverse and disorderly Others beginning to demand to be heard and beginning to chip away at the social and political power of the theorizer." These movements have a twofold task, the task of deconstruction of the colonized self and the reconstruction of "the subjectivites of the Others, subjectivities which will be both multiple and specific."[22]

Hartsock identifies subgroups in the colonizer: the colonizer who accepts (whom she argues is the modernist) and the colonizer who resists (who is the postmodernist). Someone like Michel Foucault who tries to refuse the universal/other dichotomy is the academic postmodernist who is trying to resist being a colonialist. Memmi himself as a Jewish Tunisian was familiar with both the colonizer and the colonized, and "understood only too well (the difficulty of the colonizers who refuse), their inevitable ambiguity and the resulting isolation; more serious still, their inability to act."[23] This distinction explains the difficulty of the post-Marxist today who, as a colonizer who refuses, is politically paralyzed. Some, postmodernists indeed, show a distinct tendency to social conservatism as they have effectively removed the ground on which they could act.

I think that many liberation theologians need to pay attention to Hartsock here and to recognize a mirror when it is held up to them. As academics trained largely in modernism and now often in postmodernist critique, their situation as colonizers who refuse must become clearer. Academic liberation theologians are not the poor themselves, though sometimes as female, or as racial/ethnic minorities, or as gay or lesbian, they may have outsider group status in one or more ways. But as educated, even these have some access to power in ways that the poor do not.

There is no way out of this dilemma but to return to the grassroots movement base of liberation theology and as theologians to act in solidarity with those most despised, recognizing that the step beyond the colonizer who refuses is the colonizer who becomes a traitor to his or her own colonial origins, whether that be gender for men, racial dominance for the privileged races, or class dominance for the middle and upper classes.

Traitor, because it is an uncomfortable, conflicted term, is well-chosen for this moment as we contemplate the future of liberation theology. For the liberation theologian who is educated, who has some access (however limited) to power, the temptation is always to succumb, to accommodate. Finally, albeit at first in small ways, we cease to lift up over and over and over again that those outside the church establishment, outside the academic establishment, those disenfranchised in the social and political process, are full human beings and that a full place at the table must be reserved for them.

The future of liberation theology is the future given by God: the last shall be first. And we forget this truth to our everlasting peril.

JOHN B. COBB JR.

3. Liberation Theology and the Global Economy

I was personally shocked into fundamental concern about the effects of global economic "development" by ecological awareness before I had truly understood what it was doing to the people who were being "developed." In the early days, liberation theologians in general did not share my ecological concerns, with the exception of Frederick Herzog. He was able to see that extending concern beyond the human sphere did not threaten the concern for the liberation of human beings but actually supported it.[1] Having become convinced of the primary importance of the economy in shaping the oppressions from which the world suffered, my heart still remains in continuing reflection about the dominant economy and the oppression that it causes.

The Primacy of Theology over Virtue

Herzog's deep commitment to liberation was free of defensiveness with respect to the details of a particular ideology. For that reason he could welcome into his efforts persons who came from diverse perspectives. There were no academic or theoretical tests imposed on those of us who wanted to follow him, although there always remained his own conviction of the importance of clarifying and purifying the church's dogma as well as implementing it in practice.

Like many liberal American Protestants, I found it difficult, at first, to take Herzog's emphasis on "dogma" seriously. The word is almost unredeemable for many of us because of the negative connotations of the adjective *dogmatic*. Without doubt, however, his intentions were correct. The church needs to know what it is and what it believes with the kind of clarity that directs action. Only so can it avoid simply reflecting back to a society that society's values. Herzog was particularly sensitive to this matter because of his distress at what happened in most of the German churches during the Nazi era. But he rightly saw that most churches in the American South, by whose culture I have been nurtured, were equally subservient to their society during the centuries of slavery and segregation and continuing into the time of the civil rights struggle. Truly to be the church is to hold to a clear understanding of what that means, who is the church's Lord, and what that Lord calls the church to do and be.

How different this is from what most American Christians hear in the word *dogma*! To most of us it means ancient formulations of Christian teaching whose relevance to the present is obscure and ambiguous. Furthermore, it connotes asserting these ancient formulations without listening to the confusion they cause for most hearers. The problem with the Southern churches that supported segregation did not seem to be any failure officially to subscribe to the ancient creeds. The failure, instead, was to make the right connection between their official dogma and the acute injustices in which they participated.

I have come to appreciate Herzog's convictions on this point more and more. Its importance correlates with the wrongness, from a Christian point of view, of the basic convictions and commitments of the society in which the church lives. The issue of race highlighted its importance in the South when Christians claimed that the Gospel did not require that churches be open to all. On this point there has been some progress. In Herzog's sense, the dogma is now widely accepted that racism is wrong. Now the problem in this respect is God-walk more than God-talk. Indeed, most of us have supposed that this is the typical situation, that the problem of the church is more ethical than doctrinal.

But this may, in fact, not be the case. Again and again we find that even our best-intended efforts lead us to do more harm than good. It is easy to see this when we look back to the Middle Ages and to such orgies of virtue as the Crusades. Granted the mixture of motives, we should acknowledge that the Crusades would not have occurred apart from the belief of many of the most devoted

Christians that in recovering the Holy Land from the infidels they were doing God's will. The problem was theology, not virtue.

Similarly the ill-treatment of Jews throughout most of Christian history has been due to a variety of causes. But among them Christian teaching has been a decisive factor. Many Christians have sincerely believed that for the sake of Christ the "Christ-killers" should be persecuted. The official teaching of the church supported them. The problem, again, was theology, not virtue.

In the past generation we have come to see the dark side of our missionary efforts, many of which were expressive of heroic virtue. The belief that those who did not acknowledge Jesus Christ as savior were condemned has led to attitudes toward other religions that we now recognize as false and destructive. That, in turn, led devoted Christians to actions that we cannot now condone. Again, the problem was theology, not virtue.

We have also come to acknowledge that in its teaching of the sinfulness of normal sexual feelings the church has done immense psychological harm over the centuries. Those who tried hardest to be virtuous on the whole suffered most from this teaching. Similarly, the church's official teaching about men and women has justified both the denial of women's rightful participation in many of the affairs of the world and the church and also cruelty in keeping women "in their place." The list can go on and on. In case after case, theology has guided the virtuous into evil-doing.

No doubt our theology today continues to guide us into destructive action in ways of which we are unaware. But I am more impressed currently by a point closer to that of Herzog in his appeal for attention to dogma. The church is acquiescing in the false teaching of the society in which it finds itself. By failing to articulate its own convictions clearly and employing them to criticize the dominant ideas in the wider society, it is complicit in crimes as great as those of the Southern churches with regard to racism and of the German churches in regard to Nazism.

Serving God and Mammon

The world today is organized around the service of "Mammon," that is, wealth. The New Testament is quite explicit that this service is incompatible with the service of God. Yet the church remains silent. When it speaks, it is as often in support of the service of Mammon as it is mildly critical of some of its excesses.

Of course, the service of Mammon has been a temptation throughout history. The New Testament statement would not be found there if no one in those days served Mammon rather than God. But through most of Christian history, there was no confusion in the church's teaching. To organize personal life around the pursuit of wealth was an expression of greed, one of the major vices. The function of the state or of society as a whole included the provision of needed goods and services, but it was never encouraged to subordinate all other values to this. Usually the greater temptations were self-glorification and power rather than wealth as an end in itself.

In Western Europe, in the middle of the seventeenth century the church ceased to provide the basic norms for understanding the state and society as a whole. Recognizing that divisive religious beliefs had become destructive of the well-being of the society, the churches acquiesced in the sovereignty of the state. Nationalism became the organizing principle of public life. The churches largely accepted nationalism quite uncritically and supported it, claiming God's blessing on whatever nation they found themselves in. Typically, in wars between Christian nations, Christians in both countries prayed for God's help against the other. Although some transcendence of God over nation was recognized, relatively few employed that recognition to critique the narrowness of national goals. The churches largely acquiesced in the idolatry of nationalism.

It is rare that something can become an idol without having positive characteristics and performing services for those who worship it. Certainly nations have much to commend them. They greatly reduced the fanatic strife among Christians of differing beliefs. They often brought some measure of protection to all segments of society. Over time they took over many of the services that had earlier been provided by the church in health, education, and social welfare. They served as objects of loyalty beyond the individual so that individuals could fulfill themselves in sacrificial service of a greater good than their own. But because they did this in competition or even opposition to other nations, they engaged in struggles with one another that did enormous harm. Further, as they developed competitive empires, they brought great suffering to the peoples they colonized around the world.

World War I finally awakened the churches to some extent to the idolatrous character of nationalism. As a Christian growing up between the two World Wars, I assimilated as part of Christian common sense that whereas patriotism was good, nationalism was an enemy of faith. We recognized its idolatrous character. When the most virulent nationalisms of all time emerged in Germany, Italy, and Japan, the wrong of their teaching was self-evident to many Christians. The defeat of these nations in World War II, and the global recognition of the evil that nationalism in this extreme form had done, led to the weakening of nationalism as an ideology, especially in its Western European homeland. Western Europe reorganized itself after World War II on other principles. The evil of nationalism, at least of an extreme type, is now widely recognized both in the churches and without. In the North Atlantic countries, the temptation to worship the nation has declined. When nationalism expresses itself in the former Soviet countries and in the Balkans, we find it easy to criticize and condemn. But while we condemn the sins of earlier generations, we seem blind to the analogous sin of our own time.

When Western Europe reorganized itself after World War II, it did so as an "economic community." This had great advantages. Instead of wasting resources in building up strength against one another as in the past, Europeans agreed to cooperate for the greater prosperity of all. They have been remarkably successful. They have created a situation in which it is almost inconceivable that France and Germany, whose ancient enmity drew the whole world into two great wars in this century, will again fight with one another. For this we should be profoundly grateful.

The shift of focus from national glory to economic prosperity has not been as dramatic or abrupt in North America. American nationalism had not been quite so virulent, and there was no comparable need for drastic measures to recover economically from the war. Nevertheless, American policy since World War II has been increasingly dominated by economic considerations. In part, especially in the earlier years, these included a relatively disinterested concern for the economic recovery of devastated nations and for the economic development of former colonies. But from the beginning, and increasingly in the present, the dominant concern has been the prosperity and economic power of the American people and especially of American corporations.

Economism

It is important to name this new focus of concern and commitment that has replaced nationalism as the dominant force in global history. My proposal is that we call it "economism." My thesis is that economism has become the global religion of our time, that it is idolatrous, and that Christians should name its god, wealth, as an idol.

The minimum meaning of economism is a system in which economic values are viewed as primary and therefore as properly determinative of national and international policies with only secondary concern for other values. In its present form, economism is bound up with a specific economic theory, usually called neoliberalism. For the sake of simplicity, unless otherwise specified, my further comments will be about the form of economism that is guided by neoliberal economic theory.

I have indicated that the replacement of nationalism by economism has had great advantages. These achievements give it self-evident status today and help to explain why it has wide support among Christians. But by themselves they would not have warranted subordinating all other values to the pursuit of wealth. This dominance of economic considerations required the argument that the increase of total wealth would solve a wide range of the problems human beings face.

The most plausible claim has been that the increase of wealth makes possible the overcoming of poverty without class warfare. The argument is that as the size of the pie grows, all classes benefit. In President John F. Kennedy's famous words, "A rising tide lifts all boats." It is not necessary to take from the rich in order that the condition of the poor improve. As long as the lot of the poor improves, the poor do not demand redistribution.

A second claim is that economic growth is necessary in order to generate the jobs required to keep unemployment within acceptable bounds. When growth slows, unemployment rises. When growth accelerates, companies hire.

A third claim is that as people become accustomed to freedom of action in the market, they demand also freedom to participate in political life. Hence the means of accelerating the accumulation of wealth also turn out to promote democratic political processes.

A fourth claim is that economic growth brings about a population transition. In Europe, when average income reached a certain point, families chose to have fewer children. Thus there is no need for intrusive programs to reduce population. Economic growth will slow population growth without undesirable social interference in family decisions.

A fifth claim is that economic growth will solve the problem of environmental deterioration. When average income reaches a certain point, people's concerns for the environment assert themselves, and they take the steps needed to protect it.

A sixth claim is that economic growth allows people to pursue other values as they choose. Instead of having the state determine the priority among these values, this can be left to citizens who are empowered by economic growth to express their values freely.

Together these constitute a powerful argument for the worship of Mammon instead of the Christian God. Christians should have been skeptical of such claims from the beginning. We know that idols promise more than they deliver.

Unfortunately, we have been confused by the apparently technical character of the discussion. Over a couple of centuries we have come to accept the division of knowledge among academic disciplines and the authority of experts in each field. If experts in the field of economics tell us that economic growth can accomplish all this, who are we to argue? Instead, we are glad to be relieved of dealing with the extremely difficult questions of redistributing wealth, population control, and environmental protection. We conclude that we should stand aside and allow the technocrats to work these wonders.

But those who worship God should not yield to the expertise of those who serve idols. Their virtue is not to be questioned. But because they make absolute what is finite, they are misled. When the church allows itself to mirror the dominant values of the society, it shares in this idolatry. It fails to take the opportunity to critique and expose the claims for the idol.

Economism and Liberation Theology

One of my own stimuli to criticize economism came from liberation theology. At first, I did not understand its argument that liberation should precede economic development. I thought they were both important and should both be encouraged simultaneously. But gradually I came to see what liberation theologians were telling us. Whether the economic growth, at which what is usually called development aims, benefits the people depends on who is in control. Without liberation, what is called economic development often does more harm than good.

For obvious reasons, the social theory derived from the writings of Karl Marx was the major dialogue partner for Latin American liberation theologians. Marxism was an already important factor in the societies in which liberation theology arose. Prior to liberation theology, it had been, indeed, almost the only effective expression of the aspiration of oppressed people for freedom and justice. To affirm that the Christian faith, rightly understood, stood with the oppressed in their struggle for freedom was immediately to locate Christianity on the side of Marxism against the status quo. Indeed, to side with the poor was, in many circles, to *be* a "Marxist," even if one disclaimed the label. When Christians joined Marxists in support of peasants and workers, their task was both to appreciate the Marxists and to clarify the distinctiveness of the Christian perspective.[2]

For the most part clarifying differences did not involve developing a distinct social analysis or economic theory. The distinctiveness was more often formulated in terms of belief in God, emphasis on the importance of moral and spiritual values, recognition of the universality of sin, refusal to identify the classless society with the fullness of God's purposes, more concern for the dignity of individuals, and greater hesitation about the use of violence. Christians recognized, as many Marxists did not, that a Marxist victory could lead to new oppressions, so that Christians would need to maintain a critical distance from a Marxist government as well. Thus, while Marxism in itself can function as a form of economism based on a different theory of how to bring about economic growth, liberation theology remained clear that such growth is one value among others and should not dominate over them.

The collapse of Marxism in Eastern Europe and its decline elsewhere exposed the inadequacy of the critique of Marxism by liberation theology. They exposed the fact that Marxist states have been compelled to employ terror as an instrument of government policy to a greater degree than their supporters had previously been willing to acknowledge. The thinness of support for these regimes on the part of the citizens shocked those who sought similar regimes as the solution to the problems of injustice.

In addition to this social and political failure of Marxist regimes, and closely related to it, there has been a fundamental contradiction in Marxist countries between their goal of rapid economic growth and the extensive nationalization of the economy. Nationalization necessarily means bureaucratization, and bureaucratization of the economy is inherently inefficient. This is particularly important with respect to the allocation of resources to production.

In the free market, prices are determined by supply and demand. When prices of particular commodities rise, capital flows to the production of the scarce commodities until further increase proves unprofitable. When prices fall, capital seeks more profitable uses. Hence capital is in general so invested as to meet consumer demands effectively. When prices and production quotas are set by bureaucrats, this meeting of demand does not follow. Inevitably, some commodities are produced that are not wanted and many needs go unmet.

This would happen even with perfect bureaucrats, and of course perfect bureaucrats do not exist. Actual bureaucrats are often more interested in preserving their jobs and rising in the ranks than in serving the people. They try to please their superiors and curry favor with other powerful persons. They settle for less than the best estimates of needs out of laziness or being overworked. The result is to distort the allocation of resources even more and often to delay needed decisions.

The actors in the free market are just as imperfect as the bureaucrats. We may, if we like, assume that they are morally much worse. This does not affect the comparative outcome. The difference is that their personal qualities do not prevent the free market from functioning well in the allocation of resources. The only requirements for this to happen are the rational self-interest of those who operate in the market and an adequate infrastructure. As has been pointed out over and over again, the market is the instrument whereby individual greed becomes an instrument of collective benefit. A bureaucratically administered economy, on the contrary, can function well only with the "new socialist man," and even then it cannot allocate resources efficiently.

The Global Capitalist Market

The tragedy is that the capacity of capitalism to generate faster growth than Marxism has led to a nearly complete global victory at the ideological level, a victory that is wholly undeserved. Marx himself saw that capitalism was the most effective agency of technological advance and increased production. His idea was to allow capitalism to perform its historical function and then collectivize the means of the now superabundant production owned by a handful of people. A society in which abundant goods were available for all would not require either the tyranny or the bureaucratic management that have invalidated Marxist-run societies. The demonstration that the free market grows more rapidly than the bureaucratically managed one, with less political coercion, does not invalidate Karl Marx's own ideas.

What Marx pointed out rightly was that the free market tends to concentrate wealth in fewer and fewer hands. His critique and the political power of his influence led capitalist countries to take countermeasures against this tendency. Laws against monopolies, support of labor unions, and redistribution of wealth through taxes and social services, all served to spread the wealth rather than concentrate it. Furthermore, to a greater extent than Marx anticipated, within a closed economy the increase of production makes more goods and services available to the population as a whole. As long as most experience some gain, disproportionate gains on the part of the rich are likely to be tolerated.

Now that Marxism has been discredited, however, the capitalist countries no longer find it necessary to check the concentration of wealth in fewer hands. By moving from national economies to a single global economy, they can pit the workers of one country against the workers of all others. The result is the dismantling of social services and the undermining of the power of labor unions. The system of taxation no longer needs to pretend to be progressive. In order that a national economy be "competitive," the rich must be freed from heavy taxation so as to have more to invest, and workers must accept lower standards of living and workplace safety so that production will not have to be moved to lower-wage countries with lower standards. The underclass is relegated to self-destruction and imprisonment. The increase of total production is accompanied by the increase of poverty.

Marxist critique of the distribution of wealth and income under capitalism is eminently relevant to the current scene. It is this economic maldistribution alongside the political oppression that supports it that aroused the passions of liberation theologians and drew them into alliance with Marxists. Marxist governments did in fact reduce this maldistribution, largely eliminating truly degrading poverty. This was their great accomplishment, one which deserves far more celebration than it is currently receiving. Nevertheless, the price in tyranny and inefficiency was so large that few wish to return to the Marxist system as they have known it.

The better economic models are the welfare states. These have used the market for allocating most resources, but they have used the resulting national wealth to ensure prosperity for all sectors of the population. They need not resort to tyranny. They model a situation far closer to Marx's utopian dream than has any avowedly Marxist society.

Unfortunately, these remarkable historical achievements are now under siege. The nations that followed these policies have allowed themselves to be drawn into the global economy. Competition in this economy is undermining their ability to maintain the standards they had attained when they functioned more as national economies. Per capita Gross National Product continues to rise, but income is concentrated in the hands of the few, so that the ability to provide for all the people declines.

I have focused on the operation of the economy in the First World. It might be supposed that if First World labor suffers from the globalization of the market, Third World labor must gain. Indeed, some Christian idealists have supported globalization and "interdependence" on the assumption that capitalist rhetoric about the resultant enrichment of the Third World is accurate.

Liberation theologians in Latin America were among the first to point out the failure of "development" to benefit the poor. What capitalist theorists call interdependence they rightly interpreted in terms of dependency theory: the dependence of the periphery on the center both internationally and in each country. One might suppose that, despite the loss of self-determination throughout the periphery, there would be economic gains. But this is not the case. Those who have the power also concentrate the economic gains in their own hands.

Economism and Poverty

The great success of capitalism as ideology in today's world comes from the celebration of its one great strength: its efficient allocation of resources and the resultant growth in production. Our leaders have persuaded people everywhere that this economic growth is the precondition of solving the problem of poverty without tyranny. They sometimes acknowledge that temporary sacrifices are required in order to prepare the stage for economic growth. But the basic assumption that global economic growth will benefit people in general is rarely challenged.

The oppression of people of the Third World under "structural adjustment programs," which is now being justified by these assumptions, is truly appalling, and the relative lack of protest from compassionate people in the First World is painfully astonishing. The idea that the present suffering is temporary, and that the policies that cause it will in short order begin to benefit the suffering people is honestly believed, but it is, all the same, extremely implausible for three reasons.

First, in general, economic growth has eliminated poverty only when it has been accompanied by governmental policies designed to benefit the poor. But for the sake of maximizing growth, such policies are currently being dismantled across the planet. Inevitably the resultant growth is concentrated in the hands of those who are already wealthy. In short, the elimination of poverty is hindered, not advanced, by growth-oriented policies.

Furthermore, the elimination of the most degrading consequences of poverty can be attained with little growth. I have already noted that this was accomplished in Marxist countries whose growth was minimal. Cuba today remains an example. It has been reduced to extreme poverty by the loss of Soviet subsidies and the United States' policy of isolation. But even now, in comparison with other Latin American countries, the basic needs of the poor are better met in Cuba.

The state of Kerala in India provides a more positive example in that it has attained its goals with little coercion.[3] Although its per capita income is about the same as that of India generally, it has largely eliminated extreme poverty and its most negative consequences. Unfortunately, India's new policy of entering the world market threatens this achievement.

Second, what is sought as "growth," that is, Gross National Product (or now, more often, Gross Domestic Product) has economic costs that are not subtracted from it in the standard national accounts. When a nation deforests itself, the sale of the lumber counts as economic growth. The reduction in its remaining natural resources and the many costs resulting from the environmental disruption are not subtracted. Indeed, the costs of responding to these environmental problems, such as flood control, are added to the GDP.

Or when a water treatment plant is built to replace the services of now "developed" wetlands, this adds to the GDP, although it adds nothing to the real wealth or income of the people. Increasing expenditures on police, lawcourts, and prisons add to GDP, but at best they restore a degree of safety that has been destroyed by economic changes. Economists recognize in principle that these are "defensive" expenditures, but this recognition does not affect the national accounts. If all the costs of economic growth are subtracted from the growth registered by the national accounts, there is often no real growth left. There is, therefore, no real increase of wealth in which the poor can share. The increasing wealth of the rich is at the expense of the impoverishment of others.[4]

Third, there is a still more fundamental error underlying the current global economy. This is the assumption that what is now misleadingly called economic growth can continue indefinitely. The natural resources it consumes and the capacity of nature to absorb the wastes it produces are, in fact, both finite. Technology can increase the efficiency of use and counter the production of wastes, but it cannot erase the limits. These limits will be reached long before any gains from growth trickle down to the majority of today's poor.

The current suffering of the poor across the globe, but especially in Latin America and Africa, is widely accepted even by people of good will as a necessary precursor of poor people's economic development into prosperity. Perhaps when this is recognized as the profound illusion it is, this acceptance will be withdrawn and the current idealization of the global economy will end. Perhaps there will be openness to genuine new thinking. Perhaps the passion for justice and liberation can express itself in ways that will be convincing to people of good will everywhere and we will cease to give moral support to the forces of death that now rule the world.

Refuting Other Economistic Claims

The previous section was devoted to refuting the apparently most plausible claim for economism, that it promotes the increasing economic well-being of all. In this section I will comment more briefly on the weaknesses of the other claims.

The second claim listed in the section on economism was that economic growth is essential for keeping unemployment in check. Within an economy such as that of the United States, there is some truth to this. Since we have decided not to adopt policies directly oriented to reducing unemployment, the provision of jobs depends on market activity. We are caught in a situation in which new technologies are reducing jobs so rapidly that job creation has to be quite rapid to keep up. Thus far, overall economic growth has done its work in this respect.

On the other hand, the quality of jobs is declining. Many who lose good-paying middle-management jobs through corporate downsizing cannot find comparable work. Relative job security is giving way to acute insecurity. More and more work is part-time. In short, policies geared to increasing total wealth are eroding the quality of jobs, if not their number.

In the Third World the situation is often worse. Traditional society offered some employment to most of those who needed it. Modernization undercuts that system, and unemployment often attains monumental levels. Once that has occurred, development through industrialization seems to offer the only hope. But because capital is controlled by those who have no interest in this question, huge fluctuations can occur abruptly, as capital moves in and out. To say that overall economic development has helped with regard to giving jobs to all those who want and need them is completely counterfactual.

The third claim was that the free market promotes the emergence of political democracy. It is true that a high percentage of the nations participating in the global market now have democratic governmental institutions. This may be partly because those who succeed in the market want a voice in government, as the supporters of economism argue. Partly it is because the same global powers, preeminently the United States, that support the free market also support the institutions of representative democracy and reward those who adopt them.

The question is whether these institutions really allow for significant participation of people in making basic decisions about their individual and national life. Here the answer is often negative. The global market has led to control of the local economy from distant centers, so that local governments are largely powerless with respect to economic matters. In societies organized around their economies, this leaves little of significance for the voters to decide other than whom they should elect to cooperate with global powers.

The fourth claim was that economic growth would bring the population explosion under control. This claim is heard less often today. Without slowing of population growth, it turns out that in many countries it is very difficult to increase per capita production significantly. On any realistic projection, by the time wealth grows sufficiently to affect choices about reproduction, populations will have risen to unsupportable levels. In any case, more careful studies show that family size is more affected by such factors as the roles of women in society than by average income. Furthermore, policies geared simply to economic growth typically leave large portions of the population as poor or poorer than before. Successful population policies depend on very different factors from overall economic growth.

The fifth claim was that environmental decay would be checked by economic growth. It is not false that more prosperous people can afford to give greater attention to environmental conservation. But the environmental destruction caused by policies geared chiefly to economic growth are such that long before this measure of prosperity is attained in many countries, the situation will be desperate. Indeed, environmental decay precludes the attainment of such prosperity even when that is measured by the current artificial statistics. This claim, like that about population, is heard less often today. The need to deal directly with such issues as global warming, for example, is now generally accepted.

The sixth claim is that with sufficient wealth people can pursue their other values as they wish. Like all the claims, this one has its truth. If we think of other values such as the enjoyment of music and the arts, travel, and advanced education, it is certainly true that those with sufficient economic resources have great advantages. But to justify growth-oriented policies in this way is to misunderstand the concern about the hegemony of economic values.

Economism, especially when it is guided in its policies by classical and neoliberal economic theory, promotes primary attention to self-interest defined as concern to acquire maximum goods and services with minimum effort. Although a successful market requires personal honesty, team spirit, and diligence, the econo-mistic ideology erodes such values. To say that economic growth enables people to pursue values of this sort is highly misleading. The problem cuts still deeper. Most human values depend for their transmission and nurturance on human community. But the policies adopted for the sake of promoting economic growth work consistently against traditional communities. The same is true of the nontraditional communities that grow up around new centers of economic activity. Growth is promoted by capital mobil-ity. Capital mobility means that the localities at which work is available are constantly changing. People cannot afford to put down roots.

Furthermore, community leadership is eroded. When busi-ness is largely owned locally, its leaders have a stake in the well-being of the community. When globalizing the economy leads to the control of business in distant centers of economic power, this is far less true. Those employed to run local businesses are them-selves too mobile to invest themselves emotionally in community-building.

Decline of community leads to decline of education, a decline that cannot be stemmed simply by additional expenditures. In any case, economism creates a climate in which fewer people are willing to invest their resources in community programs such as universal education. Resistance to taxes rises as human needs increase.

In these and many other ways, organizing society around the service of Mammon makes many values unattainable even for those who are most prosperous and best able to purchase what-ever the market has to offer. If a wide range of human values is to be realized, society should be ordered directly to this end. These values should include, but not be dominated by, meeting the economic needs and reasonable desires of all and providing a place for free action in the market.

M. DOUGLAS MEEKS

4. Economy and the Future of Liberation Theology in North America

One of its major progenitors, Gustavo Gutiérrez, has spoken of the finitude of liberation theology. It is only a theology. Like all theologies, it has to be questioned as to how it will continue to develop or what it will pass on to the next stages of theology. The question, of course, cannot be asked in the singular, since there is no common liberation theology. But the lasting contribution of all liberation theologies, it seems to me, is their claim that "God in the poor" is the subject matter of Christian theology.[1] To wrestle ever and again with this subject is surely the future of liberation theologies in North America. But in order to do this, liberation theologies should turn their attention more focally to economy.[2]

The first step would be for liberation theologies to realize that they need each other to speak plausibly of the redemption of threatened human beings and nature. At least in the North American academic context, the various liberation theologies have tended to nullify each other. Under narrowly construed rules of pluralism, that is, liberation theologies have so far not been able to surmount certain liberal assumptions about the spheres of knowledge and power as well as of human misery. Each liberation theology tends to concentrate on one or two spheres of oppression. This is understandable from many perspectives, but it often means that a liberation theology does not touch the complicated situations in which the poor and oppressed concretely live, even though liberation theologies methodologically require themselves to focus on the liberation of people in their actual historical situation.

The second problem is that liberation theologies have generally not yet been convincing in terms of the historical agency of liberation. The North American and Latin American practices and movements of people that liberation theologies assume as the substance of theory have often quickly dissolved, and I would argue that this is the case in large part because of conditions of economy. Liberation movements of the oppressed are not unaffected by changes in economy.[3] This is especially true in terms of the global economy at the turn of the century. Liberation theologies will therefore have to put much greater emphasis on how communities capable of being agents of liberation can be formed at all.

Furthermore, a Christian theology without the church as agency of mission to the world cannot be an effective theology. In spite of the enormously low expectations of the church in North America, liberation theologies cannot sidestep the necessity that they be theologies in relation to the actually existing churches.

Finally, liberation theologies must come to grips with the market logic itself and its effects on the church, human communities, and nature. Else they cannot realistically speak of power that can change the situation of the poor and the repression of nature. Without facing the claims of the market logic, liberation theologies shirk the true function of dogmatics.[4] Dogmatics is the church's self-examination according to the truth it confesses. It is the criticism of all decrees made by the church and the world in the name of God. Put simply, dogmatics is the church's way of making a judgment about the truth in the face of the truth claims in the church and the world that contradict Jesus Christ.

The problematics for the future of liberation theologies therefore include: (1) a greater awareness of the multidimensional character of liberation, (2) more focused attention to the historical agencies that actually bear liberation, particularly the agency of the *ecclesia*, and (3) a theoretical and practical grappling with the pervasive logic of the market in our society.

Church and Economy

Dogmatics serves the truthful speaking and living of the gospel in the world. But can the gospel be spoken publicly in North American society? Is there time and space in which the

Household of Jesus Christ can be formed in North American society? Can the gospel make any difference in creating conditions of justice and peace in North American society and the global community? These are urgent questions because the secular logics which govern the spheres of *state, economy, media,* and *technology* are so pervasive that the time and space that can be occupied by the church are frightfully meager. And without the agency of a community governed by the logic of grace we cannot speak realistically of liberation in a Christian sense.

Within these four secular macro spheres the logic of the market (the accumulation of wealth as power and commodity exchange) has become dominant, that is, even where state, media, and technology exert massive power from their own spheres, those forms of power are increasingly in service of the market logic. By market logic I mean more than the regulatory laws of economic mechanisms.[5] I mean also the cultural assumptions that shape our understanding and treatment of human beings, society, and nature. The logic of the market society has defined the ground of certainty (what can be called true and factual), what can count as the development of human beings and progress of society, and the accepted conceptions of order, rule, justice, reason, harmony, and peace. This spirit asserts itself in all spheres of sociality and increasingly proves itself as the one universal order of the world.

If, then, we connect this peculiar historical situation at the turn of the twenty-first century with the biblical narratives out of which the church must always find its identity and mission, I believe we should understand the church as a function of the "economy of God." There are many reasons the church is threatened with the loss of its reason for being today, but I suggest that in North Atlantic society the reasons come to focus in economy— not specifically in *economics* but in the ancient meaning of *oikonomia*: the relations of human beings for producing and distributing the conditions of life against death. The biblical traditions borrow this language of economy to speak of God's most inclusive relationships to creation and understand the church as a peculiar economy in service of what God is doing to redeem creation. This suggests for the church the primary metaphor of "household of Jesus Christ." The church by no means exhausts the economy of God, but if it loses its participation in the economy of God, it loses its reason for being.

In modernity, market economics increasingly displaces economy in this sense and offers itself as a pervasive logic by which all spheres of human endeavor can be comprehended and mastered. The church itself has not been spared the incursion of this logic. Indeed, the church's widespread malaise is characterized by its idolatrous absorption in this logic.

Under the assumption of the modern division of life into public and private spheres, the church has been assigned certain social responsibilities in the private sphere. It belongs to the sphere that according to G. W. F. Hegel, was left free for personal choice. The church loses its public character by submitting to the private roles defined for it by society. But the church can also cease to be public by assuming to itself the logic of the public household. Thus the church, like all other institutions in this society, has taken over—to be sure most often unwarily and indeed almost as a matter of course—the logic of market exchange as the way of gluing itself together socially and institutionally.[6] The upshot is that the church as *ecclesia* has lost its public manifestation, that is, its ability to appear in the world as an alternative economy serving God's redemption of the world.

The realities the church in the North Atlantic rim most needs are the very realities that are precluded by the market logic. Liberation in a Christian sense would include at least: (1) the public speaking of the gospel, (2) the formation of a sustained community that exists for the sake of the other, and (3) lawfully established and enforced conditions of justice and peace. The market logic, however, completely denies several realities necessary for these conditions to appear historically.

In what follows I will deal with two of these realities, namely, *praise* and *gifting*. The historical, public, and objective (spatial and temporal) appearance of these realities as defined by the narratives of God's economy I take to be the *conditio sine qua non* of Christian engagement in liberation. Though indispensable, this condition seems nearly impossible in our present society.

This is not the "fault" of the market economy. The church does not have to conform to the theology of the market (any more than it had to conform to slavery, feudal, or mercantilist logics), but so pervasive is the logic of the market as the common sense of human operations that the church will experience freedom for engagement in public liberation only as gift of God's grace.

I am not claiming that freedom from the market logic will solve all questions of the church and its mission. It won't. There are many other idolatries that face the church: racism, sexism, homophobia, repression of nature, etc. Nor am I claiming that the church must be utterly free from the market economy. Since for the foreseeable future all imaginable economics will be market-oriented, to claim that the church should be utterly free from market economy would be tantamount to claiming that the church should not even be *in* the world when in actuality the gospel claims that the church, fully present in the world, should not be *of* the world. But if the church does not manifest an alternative economy in space and time, it is not a candidate for serving God's redemption of the world.

The household of Jesus Christ is meant to be space and time filled by a Spirit with different interests, goals, and power structures than the spirit of the market society. The church is the time and space in which the coming of the Spirit of Jesus Christ under the conditions of messianic promise and discipleship creates a community devoted to the praise of God and to God's redemption of the world. The Spirit of Jesus Christ constitutes the church, gives it direction and energy, and opens up time and space for the relationships and conditions of life.

The Landscape of Liberation in North America

In the North American context two conditions have intensified since the presumed victory of market forces in 1989 that are complicating the formation of the church as a liberating community: the breakup of civil society and the escalating conflict of democracy and capitalism. These developments make it increasingly less clear in which time and space Christian liberating practice can appear.

The Shrinking of Civil Society and Denominationalism

With few exceptions North American churches have assumed the form of denomination, that is, they have not been established by the state but rather embedded in the civil society. In America the process of secularization was to some extent forestalled by the implanting of the church as denomination in civil society.

Alexis de Tocqueville observed that the genius of America lies in the institutions of its civil society, such as schools, extended families, voluntary associations, neighborhoods, arts and cultural groups, and churches. Civil society is the locus in which citizens find freedom and balm from the state and market, even if civil society and the churches are generally shaped by the spirit of state and market. Throughout their history denominations could assume the other institutions of civil society. Though the denominations were in competition with these institutions, they were nevertheless protected by them and the denominations used them for their own flourishing.[7] The positive character of denominations is that they have thereby identified with the world. The negative aspect is that denominations have often failed prophetically to believe and practice the gospel publicly.

Though American denominations originally gained their identity through their mission to "Christianize America," the functions of the "mainline" denominations in the market society have ceased to be public. They give public policy over to politics, nature to science and technology, the organizing of society to corporations and the media. They become absorbed in internal questions of meaning and purpose. They mimic the helping professions in offering coping, unburdening, and compensation for life lived in the market society; they no longer speak of redemption in biblical terms. Or they provide religious justification of public policy. But even this sparse space of appearance (therapeutic and civil religious) is now collapsing along with the rest of civil society.

North American denominations are now in a period of disorientation and cataclysmic change. We don't know whether the "fiery ordeal" they are going through is the last gasp of a denominationalism that will pass off the scene or whether they are entering a qualitatively new phase of denominationalism.[8] Denominations are collapsing from the top down, in part because they are simply running out of money. Thousands of small congregations are faced with closing and many more can no longer afford a fulltime ordained clergy person. The more they intensify the accepted market-oriented practices of the last four decades, the more ineffective denominations become. Fine-tuning of the structures or doing better what they have been doing no longer makes sense to most people. The new situation seems to be that more and more church leaders are accepting this process of demise as inevitable. In the meantime few seem to be aware how the decline of denominations is structurally implicated in the collapse of civil society. In the academic setting of theology the sign of this crisis is a kind of fatalism about the church and the disintegration of postmodern thought forms just as they are gaining widespread scholarly currency in the theological disciplines.[9] In it all, the question must be pressed, Where is the *ecclesial* agency of liberation?

The Market Society and Democracy in the North American Public Household

At the end of the twentieth century we are making decisions that will determine whether we will have a humane economy or subjugate all life to the rules of the market. Among the greatest uncertainties is the question whether democracy and capitalism can coexist.

As Karl Polanyi demonstrates, people have had to be protected from the modern market since its inception during the enclosures in England under the Tudors.[10] Market economy produces instability in community and inequality in incomes. From the beginnings of the modern market people and communities suffering from instability and income inequality have turned to the church, the institutions of civil society and, above all, the state to alleviate their suffering from the spread of the market. All democracies, in order to justify their existence, have interceded in the market with various measures to resist the rise of economic inequality.[11] Despite the massive ideological thrust to the contrary, it was democratic government, not the market, that formed the middle-class and to some extent gave access to it to the poor.

Democracy and capitalism represent two antithetical principles about the right distribution of power. The intent of democracy at its best is the systematic criticism of privilege and the inclusion of people in the public household. Democracy seeks to give all persons the dignity that is owed them because of their humanity. Therefore democracy insists on the equal distribution of political power, "one person, one vote."

Economics, as the science of the market economy, on the other hand, insists that power should rightly belong to those who win at competition in the exchange of commodities. "Driving others out of the market and forcing their incomes to zero—conquering their earning opportunities—is what competition is all about. . . . Accumulated wealth leads to income-earning opportunities that are not open to those without wealth."[12]

Democracy and capitalism have been able to coexist in North America because it has usually been possible to convert economic power into political power or vice versa, and because government could induce a more equal distribution of income by altering market outcomes.

However, with the end of state communism and the spread of the global economy, the shift in technology, transportation, and communications in the spread of the global economy has created a world where "anything can be made anywhere on earth and sold anywhere on earth." This situation has exacerbated the discrepancy between the income of the rich and the poor. Wealth is not constrained by the number of hours one can work in a day. Wealth, not limited by personal time or energy, generates wealth without an upper limit.

> Income stability is being undercut by the tectonic forces of economics. In an electronically wired village, that surge in inequality is going to be well known and perhaps even exaggerated as those with falling real incomes compare themselves with their TV neighbors who always enjoy rising real incomes. For more than twenty years earnings gaps have been rising, and for more than ten years that reality has been known with certainty. Yet the political process has yet to adopt its first program to change this reality. The problem is of course that any program that might work would involve a radical restructuring of the American economy and American society. More money is required but an aggressive program of reeducation and reskilling the bottom 60 percent of the workforce would require a fundamental painful restructuring of public education and on-the-job training. Without a social competitor, fear will not lead capitalism to include the Unincluded. Long-run enlightened self-interest should lead to the same result, but it won't.[13]

No other period in the history of North America has seen such sharply rising inequality. And the test of whether the two power systems can survive is underway. How much is the too much inequality level?[14]

The primary limit of democracy is that it requires consent but does not engender it. Democracy assumes a degree of conviviality and life resources among citizens but has no power itself to bring them into being. Democracy is at the mercy of primary communities to create the commons which are its life-setting. Participation in a common weal is the precondition of democracy, since no parent will vote on whether his or her children will eat today. Democracy "works best where it does not have to make zero-sum or negative choices because it has an expanding pie of resources to distribute."[15] But making this assumption often leads to the notion that democracy is merely the handmaiden of the market.

Our market society has constructed political systems in which economic wealth can be translated into political power. Economic power ever more facilely purchases political power, especially through the electronic media. In this situation not only the poor but also much of the middle-class populace lose interest in politics and lose confidence that government can make a difference. The poor cannot even be persuaded to vote for programs of which they will be direct beneficiaries. Cynicism about democracy and the tacit acceptance of survival of the fittest economics represent a formula for disaster.

According to Lester Thurow, the alternative to massive restructuring of our economy for the reduction of inequality is the return to a kind of feudalism that he sees already appearing in our society. From the perspective of those excluded from the public household, our society is in a downward spiral. The reason for the decline in the Middle Ages was not the forgetting of technology but rather the loss of values and abilities to organize the community on which the public household must be based. Feudalism is public power in private hands; it leads inevitably to social disorganization and disintegration.

The parallels in our time to the eight centuries of decline from the peak of the Roman Empire to the depths of the Middle Ages include: (1) the spreading of plagues such as AIDS; (2) the massive movement of immigrants flooding into the industrial world just at the time that developed countries no longer need low-skilled labor; (3) weak nations, such as Somalia, Afghanistan, Yugoslavia, and Chechenya, succumbing to feudal lords as the super power of the United States dwindles; (4) strong nations giving up federal governance to local judicatories; (5) deepening apathy and antipathy toward the growing number of homeless poor; (6) functional illiteracy spreading with decreased interest in providing for all an education that makes one a productive and responsible human being; (7) people, for reasons of security, lifestyle, exclusivity and homogeneity, moving into walled, gated and guarded communities which in turn spawn a consciousness of low interest in the *res publica* or public sphere;[16] (8) the neglect of infrastructure; and (9) growth in games of chance that exalt a lottery lifestyle and cults of superstition and hatred.

When these things happened in the Middle Ages, everyone had to attach himself or herself to a feudal lord who provided both state functions of defense, law, and order, as well as employment. Feudal barons thus had the right to control all aspects of the individual's life, work, housing, reproductive rights, and justice.

No one can foresee the consequences in our society if inequality of incomes and instability continue to escalate. But neither the market economy nor democracy can long exist in a climate of hostility. The task of the church in this situation is to contribute to creating the basic community in which the values and practices that support an economy of life are engendered. The church has no other way of doing this except through its own reculturing by the gospel and the sacraments of God's *oikonomia*.

Church as Alternative Economy

We have seen that the church has been to a large extent absorbed into the market society and is itself in significant ways organized according to the market logic. Can we speak concretely of the presence of God in the Spirit making room and time for the embodiment of the church so that it can actually appear publicly and make a historical difference?

How can the church block the spread of the totalistic tendencies of the market so that, dwelling in God, it can be an alternative *oikonomia*? Is it possible for the church to embody the logic of grace as opposed to the logic of the market so that it manifests alternative forms of property, work, and consumption?

Unless we are focused on the formation and reformation of ecclesial community, the churches have little actual means to address in any significant public way the transformation of the economic and political subjugating realities that are causing massive human misery in the global community.

Surely it is folly to consider liberation in a Christian sense if we are not asking how disciples, evangelists, stewards, and missionaries who can practice liberation can be formed. The ancient construal of *economy* included questions of how to form and sustain community, questions of how the members of the household are related to each other. The impoverishment of modern economics is its exclusion of these questions. Recently it has become commonplace to ask whether there are any communities that can nourish democratic values or that can bear politics.[17] Our question is to what extent there can be any genuine communities of transformation in the church.[18]

In all of this it is important to remember that Christian theology aided in the invention of the secular. It, too, has often uncritically assumed the logics of secular reason implicit in politics, economics, sociology, and psychology.[19] Secular logics offer a universal foundation to replace faith. Christian theology has been a poor contender with the other logics, and the more it assumes them, the less it is needed.

My claim is that the future of liberation theology in North America lies in the arduous work of creating actual human communities of liberation through praise and gifting. I conclude with some preliminary reflections on how praise and gifting fund the alternative economy of *ecclesia* as it becomes home for the poor and as it funds liberation in the public household.

Praise and the Economy of Abundance

The participation of Christians in the liberation of those who suffer oppression of any kind depends upon the gospel being spoken, heard, and believed publicly. The gospel must be able to stand against the other public truth claims that demand loyalty and compliance. Modern theology has demanded that the gospel meet the tests of intelligibility, plausibility, and relevancy according to enlightened epistemological standards; this has resulted in the tendency to apply the gospel to ever smaller spheres of truth and power. As we enter a new world of cyberspace wired for instant communication, reading and speaking the gospel will certainly be under an even greater stress of increasing docetism.[20] How can the gospel withstand the totalizing claims of market society?

This is not just an epistemological question. It is a spiritual question. Liberation theology would need to develop then what Frederick Herzog called a "critical spirituality." I submit that the spiritual presupposition of the market logic is scarcity.[21] The totalizing dominance of the market logic rests on the claim that there is not enough to go around and that human desire can never be satisfied. If all human logics and operations stem from this assumption, the gospel can be no more than comfort for loss and lack and has no power against the life of conflict and competition that scarcity engenders.

Modern market theory cannot function without scarcity as a presupposition. And scarcity has usually been associated with selfishness, greed, austerity, sensuality run amuck, or a greed taking advantage of others. Recently Peter L. Danner has attempted to "humanize" scarcity by redefining scarcity as inherent in the human being.[22] But this represents an uncritical spiritualization of scarcity. Danner seeks to demonstrate that scarcity is merely a basic dimension of the human person.[23] Scarcity, as it turns out, is nothing but what springs from human desiring or hoping. If we but attend to the basic structure of human reality, we shall discover that human "wants and hopes transcend their material means."

Scarcity then is the constant human attempt to make material and spiritual means meet. It is the "spiritualization of human wanting" by which "persons as embodied spirits use the matter which binds them to the here and now to transform it into something more akin to spirit."[24] The problem of making ends meet, of wants pushing beyond the means to have, is "embedded in the human person and fundamental to the human condition."[25] The soaring of the human spirit meets the paltry material resources of this "poor little earth," and the result is the vast engine of production which catches up, at least theoretically, the whole human race in meeting the resulting human needs. Indeed, it sounds much more humane to speak of scarcity as the "effort to transcend the material," which drives the economy.

Danner lodges scarcity ("making ends meet") in the spirit of human desiring. No matter what goods human beings have, they are never fully satisfied. So far, "scarcity" seems not different from Augustine's famous prayer, "O God, our hearts are restless until they find their rest in you," that is, at least in the sense in which he speaks of scarcity as the infinite self-transcending of human existence. But Danner then goes on to connect scarcity with *pricing*, though this crucial part of his argument is somewhat downplayed. Scarcity, once pricing is introduced, is still the condition of human beings having to decide among different means in order to fulfill a desire. Here he jumps a vast divide that, according to Karl Polanyi, puts him in the land of the *formal* economy as opposed to the *substantive* economy and makes him a proponent of the former according to which the discussion of scarcity leaves the concrete situation of meeting daily needs ("give us this day our daily bread") and enters a field of logically construed scarcity.

Pricing still gives us a formal, scarcity economy consisting of "scarce means under conditions that induce acts of choice among different uses of insufficient means. . . ."[26] But insufficiency of means, according to what seems to me Polanyi's incontrovertible argument, does not imply choice or scarcity. It does not induce choice unless two other conditions are given: (1) more than one use for the means (otherwise there is nothing to choose from) and (2) more than one end with an indication of which of them is preferred. The *substantive* meaning implies neither choice nor insufficiency. Human "livelihood may or may not involve the need to choose. Custom and tradition, as a rule, eliminate choice, and if choice is there, it need not be induced by the limiting effect of a 'scarcity' of means."[27]

In a more theological vein Danner acknowledges the corruptibility of the human spirit's desiring—but not adequately. According to Paul, human desiring is regularly "sold into slavery to sin. . . . For I do not do what I want, but I do the very thing I hate. I can will what is right but I cannot do it. . . . For I do not do the good that I want, but the evil I do not want is what I do" (Rom. 1:15, 18-19). I have everything I could possibly need and yet still cannot decide for the good. The painfulness of making a wrong choice may be caused as much by surfeit of means as by insufficiency of means.

At the heart of the scriptural *oikonomia tou theou* (economy of God) is this subversive claim: "The Lord is my shepherd, *I shall not want.*" The strange logic of the *oikonomia tou theou* does not begin with scarcity but with abundance, even superabundance. If the *righteousness* of God (God's power for life against death) is present and trusted, then there is enough for God's will to be done, for the *oikonomia tou theou* to be established. Then it is possible realistically to speak of hungering and thirsting after "more and better" being transformed into hunger and thirst for God's righteousness, which is a deeply satisfying, finite fulfilling.

This "economy" is obviously qualitatively different from the logic of the market reflected in neoclassical economics. It refers to what God does to create the conditions of home in creation so that all of God's creatures will have access to the conditions of life against death. It does not deny that there are natural and human lacks and insufficiencies, but it does deny the notion that scarcity creates a situation of choosing among various means. In other words, it denies "formal" scarcity, a scarcity created by the logic of choosing among scarce means. God makes possible all things necessary for doing God's will: "My grace is sufficient." What is infinite is not human desiring but God's grace. Without doubt this faith looks like foolishness to the world. But it is the *conditio sine qua non* of what is expected to be the objective, historical *oikonomia tou theou* occupying time and space.

From this perspective economy would not depend on spiritualizing material wants. It would recognize pricing as quite appropriate to commodities but would reject Danner's notion of universal pricing. The humanizing element would stem from quite a different source than universal, infinite spiritual desiring for "more and better." It would arise instead from a shared communal understanding of social goods. If something is a commodity, it should be submitted to pricing and exchange. But if something is necessary for life, it may not be a commodity and therefore should be free from pricing and exchanging.

An example of this is found in the biblical history of bread, in which Pharaoh's bread and the manna are radically contrasted as "commodity" and "gift" and in which the eucharistic bread is elevated and given a new, shared communal meaning: "This is my body." This social good may not be priced or exchanged because it is not a commodity. Hunger unto death and the joy of the "bread of life" are no situations for pricing, for there are no alternative means or ends. The bread of life is the occasion for the praise of God's abundant gifting, which makes life whole even in the face of insufficiency and undermines artificial, formal scarcity.

Like the rest of culture in the North Atlantic rim the church is affected by the numbing experience of artificial scarcity and satiation. The effect of the practice of scarcity-based market logic is satiation. Both scarcity and satiation deaden the spirit and impede communal life with the other. Artificial scarcity spawns the lottery culture: The others may not make it, but I may. Satiation slakes the thirst for righteousness. Scarcity and satiation leave only one possibility for the distribution of what is necessary for life and life abundant: the logic of exchange. The genuinely other cannot appear in this logic, nor can the reality of grace. Praise opens up time and space for liberation because it breaks the stranglehold of other logics. Praise opens up space and time for the alternative logic of the gospel by attesting truth worthy to be trusted: The source of life is the abundance of God's love, not the urge to fill the void and not conflict over the "not enough." The deepest desire of life is to acknowledge the glory of God's power for life.[28] Praise breaks the ontic grip of fate and death and creates a space of freedom in which the creature can conform to the glory, shalom, and goodness of God. Praise is the biblical realization that the *oikonomia tou theou* is based on the plenitude, the abundance of God's grace instead of scarcity. Praise is the recognition of God's beauty and thus introduces the aesthetic as foundation of the epistemological.[29]

All freedom which is not based on freedom from idolatry is on the way to another slavery. Praise is freedom from idolatry; as such, it is the fundamental freedom that God gives. Praise entails naming God and the gods. Praise is the free space and time in which it is known what must not be believed and trusted.[30]

Jubilate, doxology, *hosanna* are the response to God's act of grace already accomplished, which can only be acknowledged, but praise is also hoping, expectation of what God has not yet done, of what is still coming. The evangel evokes praise as trust in God's faithfulness to God's promise. Praise creates the time in which one would otherwise have to justify self, deal with one's guilt, and prove one's immortality. Praise cuts short the disengagement and alienation implicit in self-creation. Praise thus creates the time and space in which power can be redefined as God's power of suffering and God's power against suffering. God's suffering creates the recognition of differences. Praise is the acknowledgment of the real presence of Jesus Christ in the stranger, the poor, the homeless and the nameless. By opening up space and time for the "law of grace" and the logic of forgiveness, praise creates the conditions for the economy of shalom instead of conflict, the economy of mutuality instead of mastery and control.

Peace and Justice:
The Eucharistic Community of Gifting

The economy of God lives from the time and space created by God's promises to creation and our promises to God and each other. Christian life is baptismal existence. Making, giving, receiving, and keeping promises constitute the historic genesis of the church. Promising is the means by which the Holy Spirit constitutes the church. Promising is the social energy and dynamism by which the church perdures through time. A liberating community depends on baptismal promise and thus seems foreign to a society of contract. How can the baptismal community of mission come into being in such a society?

This leads us to a consideration of the peculiar character of the "economy" of the household of Jesus Christ in which God's love as gift is embodied in relation to the stranger, thereby breaking through the fixations and sediments of society and creating new time and space for community.

The ecclesial community formed at the Lord's Table is the engendering locus of the alternative economy of the household of Jesus Christ. The viability of the church's liberating work for justice and peace in North America will depend on whether it can become a gifting community in a commodity society where gift becomes increasingly problematic.[31] God's household of praise and promise lives eucharistically.[32] The eucharist concretizes God's being as love in terms of gifting relationships as opposed to commodity exchange relationships.

The eucharist blocks the logic of exchange and creates a new reciprocity or mutuality of giving. Eucharistic oikic relationships create the space and time in which we may be gifted and give ourselves. It is an economy in which God's gifting of Godself gives us room to give.

The internal life of the Triune God is both a picture and the fount of the coherence, structure, and substance of Christian generosity. This view of the Trinity opens up the possibility of thinking God's being through the hyperbolic logic of giving. The gratuity of God's giving is the mystery of God's being. God creates out of the diffusion of goodness, not an act of free will. This fecundity is at once God's withdrawal to give space to God's creatures and God's indwelling in God's creation. The Trinity is the community of extravagant, overflowing, and self-diffusive goodness. The gift is nothing other than Godself. God's being as love is essentially other-related, ecstatic, and passionate. Primordial giving follows the passion that inlays the act of giving. God's being as love seeks affiliation, a society of individual persons who are both free and connected through acts of excessive and mutual giving.

What kind of economy does God embody and encourage? The biblical narratives point to God's overwhelming generosity to human beings and the creation. God's hyperbolic giving initiates all our giving. The gift always precedes the act of passing it along. But God's love should not be made so transcendent and idealized that God's gratuity excludes human giving in return.[33] Response to God's giving should not be the logic of exchange, but God's giving does create more than gratitude. It creates human mutuality and further giving. Giving is the way in which God must be received. God aims at a community that responds to giving with further giving, creating relationships of obligation and responsibility. God's excess creates space and time for human reciprocity. Being a Christian means being involved in a structure of demands and benefits.

A commodity is truly consumed when it is sold because nothing about the exchange assures its return. The peculiar reality of gifting, however, is that when the gift is used, it is not used up. The gift that is passed along remains abundant. Gifts that remain gifts can support an affluence of satisfaction, even without numerical abundance.[34] Gifting replaces the bloated satiety that results from narcissistic consumption and competition for scarce goods with the liberating fulfillment that stems from sharing.

JÜRGEN MOLTMANN

5. Political Theology and Theology of Liberation

My treatment of this subject is not from the perspective of a neutral observer but rather from that of a participant. I understand this chapter as a contribution to the dialogue that has gone on from the very beginning and that must now, in view of changed relationships in Europe, begin anew. With the passing of the Second World, the Third and the First find themselves facing the necessity of defining a new relationship to each other. My own context is Europe and, within Europe, Germany. I speak about liberation theology from the perspective of European political theology. Many Latin American liberation theologians share the judgment of Gustavo Gutiérrez that there is a "gap" between the "progressive theology" of the modern world and the liberation theology of those who suffer oppression at the hands of this modern world. European political theology is understood as an academic theology, whereas Latin American liberation theology is viewed as a theology of the people. As one who is affected by this judgment, I want to examine it. I will trace the history of political theology in order to demonstrate that it is precisely not a "progressive," liberal theology of an established middle class but rather a politically and socially critical theology of those who are victimized by the First World, and that it can therefore be a natural ally of Third World liberation theology.

Origins and Beginnings

Theology of liberation and political theology originated at approximately the same time, in the years 1964–1968, but in completely different circumstances: liberation theology among the poor in Latin America, political theology in the context of the cold war in a divided Europe. Liberation theology emerged from the human conflict between North and South, political theology from the conflict between East and West in the northern hemisphere.

Latin America was at that point a continent beginning to break out of its centuries-old colonial and economic dependence on Europe and North America. The successful socialist revolution in Cuba under Fidel Castro in 1959 provided the starting signal, picked up far and wide, for the rise of "popular fronts" in many Latin American countries and for Christian participation in them. Early theological interpretations of this dynamic eruption were groping attempts to determine the future. The educated class and those striving to move up the economic and social ladder took over the development programs of the First World nations, and their theologians spoke of a "theology of development." As it became increasingly clear that the development of some was being paid for by the exploitation of others, however, this scheme disappeared and was replaced by the "theology of revolution" proclaimed by Richard Shaull at the Church and Society Conference in Geneva in 1966, and embodied by Camilo Torres in Columbia in his life and death.[1] The revolution, which brings about justice for the oppressed people, was for Torres a necessary dimension of Christian love of neighbor. The goal of the political revolution, however, was socialism as an alternative to the capitalism under which the people had suffered. While Salvador Allende was in power in Chile, the movement "Christians for Socialism" came into being and had its famous conference in 1972 in Santiago de Chile. With the publication of Gustavo Gutiérrez's epochal book in 1972 *The Theology of Liberation* had established itself.[2] In its negative aspect the formulation is clear but in its positive aspect it is open: Liberation assumes actual economics, political and cultural oppression, and has as its goal a life of freedom and justice. It speaks of an historical process, not of a condition. The process of liberation is carried out by the "popular front," that is, a movement originating among the common people. Theology is the reflection of this movement in light of the gospel. Theology of liberation is located in, and determined by, a specific context and consciously chooses to be so located and determined. The suffering of the poor is its *locus theologicus*, its "*Sitz im Leben*" or social location. Participation in the peoples' movement precedes theology: first orthopraxis, then orthodoxy! The church participates in the popular movement by virtue of its "preferential option for the poor." Liberation theology utilizes sociological analysis to uncover the causes of poverty, for example, the theory of dependence, a corollary of Vladimir I. Lenin's theory of imperialism. It no longer distinguishes between world history and salvation history, but testifies rather to the whole salvation of the whole world. Liberation theologians formulated the better texts of the Latin American Bishops Conference in Medellín in 1968 and in Puebla in 1979 and thereby involved the church itself in the transformation of Latin America.

Europe also had become a restless continent during the decade of the 60s. The cold war became increasingly critical following the erection of the Berlin wall in 1961. The iron curtain separating East and West became impermeable. West and East Germany became parade grounds for the greatest concentration of military power in the world: in addition to two German armies, four foreign ones confronted each other, both sides armed with more than 12,000 nuclear warheads. Anti-communism on the one side and anti-capitalism on the other completely dominated the respective political ideologies and made any internal opposition impossible. People lived in two distinct and opposing camps. The first sign of hope came from the West European social democracy—Willy Brandt: "Risk more democracy!"—and from Czechoslovakian reform communism—Alexander Dubcek: "Socialism with a human face!" From both movements arose the first attempts to overcome the deadly division of Europe, to demilitarize the continent, and to build a "common house for all of Europe." The "political theology" of Johann Baptist Metz, Helmut Gollwitzer, Dorothee Sölle, Jan Lochman, and myself had its origins in this historical situation and was a theology intentionally critical of ideology and society.[3] But why was it called "political" theology?

The new political theology was born in Germany following the Second World War and under the shock of Auschwitz. Those of us who began our theological work after the war were painfully conscious of the fact that we could not escape living in the shadow of the Jewish holocaust. "After Auschwitz" became for us the specific context for theology.[4] The long shadows of this historic guilt became our *locus theologicus*. We associated with the name Auschwitz not only the moral and political crisis of our nation but a theological crisis of Christian faith as well. Why had Christians and church leaders, with few exceptions, been silent? It was not for lack of personal courage. We discovered in our Protestant and Catholic traditions patterns of behavior which led to that failure: (1) The middle-class opinion that "religion is a private matter" and has nothing to do with politics. This privatizing of religion led to the secularization of politics. Christians who abhorred Adolf Hitler and lamented the fate of the Jews went into an "interior emigration" and in this way preserved their personal innocence. (2) The separation of religion and politics by means of the (misleading) Lutheran doctrine of the two kingdoms. By means of this separation, religion and conscience were confined to the church, and society was turned over to an unscrupulous politics of power. "One cannot rule a state with the Sermon on the Mount," Otto von Bismarck had said, and he had promised Germans instead "blood and iron." The new political theology presupposes the public witness of faith and the political discipleship of Christ. It does not aim at "politicizing" the churches, a frequently made accusation, but seeks rather to "christianize" the political existence of churches and Christians according to the standard of Christian discipleship given in the Sermon on the Mount. Political life is the context for Christian theology, which is critical with respect to political ideologies and the civil religion of those in power, and affirming with respect to the concrete engagement of Christians on behalf of justice, peace, and the preservation of creation.

The first contours of this political theology began to emerge in the Christian-Marxist dialogue, organized in those years by the Catholic Society of St. Paul: 1965 in Salzburg, 1966 in Herrenchiemsee, and 1967 in Marienbad, Czechoslovakia.[5] These were unforgettable encounters between reform Marxists and reform theologians, between revolution-inclined Christians and Marxists pursuing religious questions. We came from eastern and western Europe, "from anathema to dialogue," and "from dialogue to cooperation" as Roger Garaudy put it.[6] Political theology became the first post-Marxist theology, that is, a theology which had worked through Ludwig Feuerbach's and Karl Marx's critique of religion and idolatry and, in response to the challenge of Marxist social criticism, translated into the present the passion of Jesus for the poor. The transmission of the best elements of Marxism and of Christian theology was greatly aided by Ernst Bloch with the book, *The Principle of Hope* (1986; German 1959).[7]

This was the way things stood as the year 1968 unfolded. For liberation theologians it was a year of victory, for they succeeded in this year in decisively influencing the documents of Medellín. For those engaged in political theology it was a year of defeat: in the fall of 1968 Soviet President Leonid Breschnev ordered Warsaw Pact troops to invade Czechoslovakia and with brutal force put an end to "socialism with a human face." This led to the death of the Protestant theologian Joseph Hromadka, and the Marxist philosopher Viteslav Gardavski was interrogated and tortured to death. The names of participating theologians, including my own, were put on the lists of the states' security services. Labeled as "CIA agents, anarchists, and theorists of synthesis," we were banned from socialist countries. Books, writings, quotations, and citations were subject to censorship. I am supposed to have said at that time: "The lights in Europe are now going out for 20 years." It lasted precisely 21 years!

Developments in European Political Theology

Neither "liberation theology" nor "political theology" designate a single uniform theological movement. Both are generalizations, sharing a common orientation, but embracing great diversity. Thus what I now present as developments in "political theology" represent only my view of things.

Socialist Theology

The year 1968 also saw the high point of the student revolts in Paris and Berlin, in Berkeley, Tokyo, and Mexico City. It was a youth rebellion, a cultural revolution, a radical democratic and a socialist movement, and much more. In April 1968 student leader Rudi Dutschke was shot in Berlin. From the student movement in Berlin emerged the socialist theology of Helmut Gollwitzer.[8] Gollwitzer was a student of Karl Barth and, since the time of the Confessing Church in the Third Reich, politically engaged. He was familiar with Marxism and the Soviet system as a result of his ten years as a prisoner of war in Russia. Nevertheless it was the students who first convinced him of the reality of capitalism's "crimes against humanity" and the necessity of a revolution encompassing all of life. In numerous writings after 1968 he portrayed capitalism as a "revolution" under which humanity would perish unless there could be a return to life. In this conversion from destructive greed to love of life he saw the reign of God breaking into this distorted world. His "Theses on Revolution as a Theological Problem" were passed from hand to hand in those days. Gollwitzer saw in capitalism a life-threatening contradiction to the reign of God and in socialism—according to Barth—an actual parable corresponding to, and actualizing in a preliminary way, the coming reign of God. His "Challenges of Conversion" are "Contributions to a Theology of Society" (1976). His "Capitalistic Revolution" (1974) brings together the gospel and the social revolution and seeks a credible place for the church in the class struggle. His major work of this period, *Krummes Holz—aufrechter Gang: Zur Frage nach dem Sinn des Lebens* (1970), places the individual aspects of this revolutionary process in the wider context of theology and its life connections. Gollwitzer's socialist theology was similar to the "theology of revolution" of Camilo Torres, whom he also cited in support of his position. In those years Gollwitzer was not only a pioneer of thought for students engaged in the socialist cause but was also the spiritual advisor for many involved in the student movement.

Theology of Peace

The year 1968 also marked the beginning of worldwide protests against the Vietnam war. The protests were closely connected to the student revolts: "Make love not war!" Mass demonstrations took place in all the major cities in the West and in Asia and led to the decision of the U.S.A. in 1973 to end the war. With the end of the Vietnam war the interest of the superpowers was again focused on Europe and the arms race on both sides began, primarily in both parts of occupied Germany. This led to increased resistance by the German peace movement. The movement had in the 50s strongly protested the rearming of West Germany and the deployment of atomic weapons: "Fight nuclear death!" In the late 70s the Americans stationed Pershing 2 rockets and cruise missiles in West Germany and drafted plans for a war against the Soviet Union in Europe. In East Germany the Russians stationed their SS-20 rockets. The climax of the peace movement came in 1983 when 100,000 people formed human chains throughout West Germany in nonviolent protest, but the German government nevertheless carried out instructions of the United States against the majority opinion of the citizens. Governments in those days discussed "security"; in the churches and among the people the topic of discussion was "peace." In the Christian churches opinion was divided: some defended nuclear weapons as essential for guaranteeing peace, others were prepared "to live without weapons." In 1982 the Reformed Church declared that the system of nuclear deterrence was incompatible with Christian faith and proclaimed the *status confessionis*.[9] The Evangelical Church in East Germany formally "renounced" the "spirit, the logic, and the practice of nuclear deterrence." A strong peace movement developed in East Germany and led to the peaceful revolution of 1989. Peace theologians of the movement were Provost Heino Falcke in Erfurt and Joachim Gastecki, who now chairs Pax Christi. Only the Catholic Bishops Conference and the Evangelical Church of Germany (EKD) were of the opinion that Christians could be for or against the system and that the church was there for people on either side of the issue.

1983 became the year of the Sermon on the Mount in West Germany. The Christian peace movement appealed to the Sermon on the Mount to justify its nonviolent work in the service of peace. Politicians and political parties tried their hand at biblical exegesis. Major newspapers printed the Sermon on the Mount on the front page. During this period political theology took concrete form in the theology of peace and provided protest movements and actions of civil disobedience with theological legitimization. Spirits as diverse as Gollwitzer and Sölle, Käsemann and Greinacher found themselves involved in the peace movement.[10] In a situation of "structural violence" such as in Latin America one would answer the question of violence differently, but in Europe only nonviolent actions were credible. Only the strict abstention from violence in the German revolution in East Germany led to the fall of the forced socialist system.[11]

Ecological Theology

The origin of environmental consciousness and the beginning of the "green" movement are impossible to date with precision. After Rachel Carson's *Silent Spring* had led in the late 60s to the formation of research commissions in the U.S., the Club of Rome study, *The Limits of Growth* (1972), brought the problem into worldwide consciousness. Environmental catastrophes multiplied, damaged oil tankers poisoned the coastlines, the chemical industry in Basel destroyed all life in the Rhine river, acid rain led to dying forests in the Black Forest, gases from industry and auto traffic and methane gas from the rice fields led to the disintegration of the ozone layer in the atmosphere, and, finally, the Chernobyl disaster in 1986 rendered wide stretches of White Russia uninhabitable for centuries to come and has led to the death of 150,000 people thus far. Everywhere groups formed spontaneously to protect nature from destruction at the hands of human beings. Greenpeace and the "green" parties in Europe are the best known representatives. The churches throughout the world were confronted with the problem through the address of the Australian biologist John Birch at the meeting of the World Council of Churches in Nairobi in 1975. Most of the regional churches in Germany hired "environmental pastors" in order to propagate in the churches a lifestyle that is more considerate in its relationship to nature. While modern scientific and technical civilization began with the conquest of nature 400 years ago and justified it on the basis of the biblical affirmation that human beings were created to "have dominion" over the earth, Western Christianity must share in the blame for the way the development has gone. Only a reformation of the religious and moral values of the Western world can rescue nature and secure the survival of humankind. The first "ecological theology" originated in the U.S. with the process theologian John Cobb, and Gerhard Liedke, an Old Testament scholar in Germany who wrote *Im Bauch des Fisches: Ecological Theology* (1979). This was followed by a series of ecclesiastical manifestos on "Reconciliation with Nature" and the rise of a new creation spirituality. I myself joined that movement with my own ecological doctrine of creation in *God in Creation* (1985). Like socialist theology and peace theology, so also ecological theology wants to move Christians to participation in such movements and to realize their own vision within them. On the other hand it, like them, brings societal problems into the church in order that the church might be present in the contradictions and sufferings of humanity and nature.[12]

Theology of Human Rights

A less noticeable but nonetheless important dimension of political theology in Europe can be seen in theological reflections on human rights. In 1977, following seven years of study, the World Federation of Reformed Churches agreed on a "Theological Declaration on Human Rights." One year later a similar study by the Lutheran World Federation appeared. And already in 1974 the Papal Commission, *Justitia et Pax*, had published a declaration on "The Church and Human Rights."[13] All these declarations base the "dignity of persons," which is to be neither surrendered nor destroyed, on the image of God which they embody. Thus faith in God is united with respect for human beings. They all seek a balance between individual human rights as these are spelled out in the United Nations "General Declaration on Human Rights" of 1948 and social and economic human rights as these were agreed upon in the "Human Rights Treaty" of 1966. In terms of practical consequences all three declarations push for the linkage of politics, domestic and foreign, with human and civil rights. This had significant consequences in the 1970s: in the Latin American military dictatorships, as in the Eastern European party dictatorships, groups sprang up advocating human and civil rights. We have them, above all, to thank for the bloodless overthrow of that dehumanizing dictatorship we have experienced. In Europe these groups and movements brought about the resolutions of the CSCE conferences which began with Helsinki in 1975. Human and civil rights have thus become the constitutional foundation for the "common House for all of Europe."

Groups of ecumenical theologians and lawyers are today working with the U.N. on expanding human rights by means of a declaration of the rights of future generations and the rights of nature to be included in an "Earth Charter" commissioned by the U.N. in Brazil in 1992.

Feminist Theology

Political theology did not produce a feminist theology, but the new feminist theology understands itself as a "political theology."[14] The feminist movement in general, which seeks the liberation of the woman from patriarchal oppression and the full recognition of human rights for women, began in the U.S., although it can be traced back to impulses originating in the French Revolution. In 1974 the World Council of Churches organized a conference in Berlin aimed at overcoming sexism in culture and church. In 1978 the first ecumenical conference on feminist theology took place in Brussels, and in 1979 the ecumenical consultation on the new partnership between men and women in the church was held in Sheffield. Many church synods have taken up this theme since then with varying degrees of success. Feminist theology is political insofar as it offers theological vision and reflection for a comprehensive cultural revolution, which will be carried on initially by women themselves. It functions in a critical way to bring into the light of public scrutiny the kind of daily brutality and humiliation that go on secretly in families and between men and women. The new women's shelters speak for themselves. It is also a human and civil rights movement for women in society and in churches. Finally, feminist theology also motivates Christian women to take part in the general feminist movement on the one hand, and on the other hand introduces these questions into the churches, which are even more strongly dominated by patriarchy than society is, not to mention the refusal of the Roman Catholic and Orthodox churches to ordain women.

Where Do We Stand?

Let's look at the balance sheet.

(1) Political theology is not a purely academic theology but rather a theology related to the expectations and experiences of praxis groups and protest movements of the populace of European countries. In this respect it is kindred to Latin American liberation theology even though under very different circumstances.

(2) Political theology is not to be identified with "progressive theology," whether that of liberal Protestantism or of modern

Catholicism. The differences between the conservative Protestant Wolfhart Pannenberg and myself, or between the political theologian Johannes Baptist Metz and the progressive postmodernist Hans Küng are obvious. Those theologians have never taken part in our causes and conflicts, instead they have often even fought against us. Liberal theology was and is the theology of the established middle class. Political theology has its evangelical roots in the anti-establishment theology of Karl Barth and in the resistance experiences of the Confessing Church. In the early peace movement of the 50s we always missed Rudolf Bultmann and his liberal students. Political theology, as I understand it, is the true dialectical theology: a theology of contradiction and hope, of the negation of the negative and the utopia of the positive.

(3) Political theology in the First World has always taken a *critical* position over against the self-justifications of those in power. Drawing on Christian memory of the suffering and death of Christ under the violent power of the Roman Empire acting through Pontius Pilate, we have always attempted, in the name of its victims, to deprive those who rule by force of their legitimization. We have taken a critical stance over against "political religion," "civil religion" with its ideology of patriotism, the "Christian West," and "anti-communism." We have striven to "demythologize" the political and economic powers.

(4) Political theology has always attempted—as I have shown—to speak on behalf of the "victims of violence" and to be the public voice for those who have no voice: in socialist theology for workers, in peace theology for the (potential) victims of an atomic war in Europe and for the (actual) victims of the arms race and weapons export in the Third World, in the theology of human rights for those deprived of dignity and rights in east European dictatorships, in feminist theology for exploited and mistreated women, and in ecological theology for the plundered creation. If liberation theology focuses on *one* theme, the liberation of the poor, political theology focuses on *multiple* themes, but it always has to do with liberation of the victims and critique of the victimizers.

(5) Political theology lives in the various praxis groups and contemporizes the revolutionary traditions of the Bible and Christian history. That is the message of Jesus regarding the reign of God, which comes to the poor and the children of this

world, not to those at the top of the ladder of human "progress" but to the victims of human violence. The Christian socialism of Ragaz and Kutter, of Blumhardt and Heimann, was the first to comprehend this. There is, moreover, the closeness of Jesus to the sick and the lepers of his society. Even today this attracts persons to Jesus and draws Christians to the victims of this society. And there is, finally, the Sermon on the Mount as the constitution of the reign of God in this world. It has become for many of us the master plan for peace in a violent world. To summarize: without a doubt, it is the intention of our political theology to transform persons from degraded objects at the mercy of external forces into free subjects of their own lives. In November 1989 we experienced in East Germany that a people that had been dominated and humiliated for 40 years rose up and brought down not only a government but an entire system with the confident cry: "We are the people," for "all power comes from the people." This experience of liberty is what we wish also for people who live under the tyranny of a "free market" economy.

(6) It is good to be related to one's own context in order to remain specific. In this sense, some are Europeans, others are Latin Americans. It is a mistake, however, to turn theology into a provincial enterprise by saying: liberation theology is good for Latin America, political theology is good for Europe, black theology is good for blacks, feminist theology is good for women. Every theology is *contextually* conditioned, of course, but every theology is *theology* and to that extent *universal* and must be taken seriously. Moreover, every context is connected to every other context, whether unilaterally by virtue of domination or mutually by means of shared interests. Every theology stands under the directive: think globally—act locally! To this extent liberation theology is just as global as political theology must claim to be. But how do they relate to each other?

The New Situation: Open Questions

The modern world of North Atlantic society has lived since 1492 at the expense of nature and the peoples of Latin America. The suffering that takes place there is, in fact, the underside of that very history which we experience from the topside. This applies to the exploitation of the raw materials of nature as well as to the exploitation of cheap labor and the encumbering of nations with debt. Starting points for a "liberation of the oppressors" are to be found in the political theology presented above. Such theology is part of the internal critique of the contradictions of the "modern world" under which the Third World suffers most. Now that the Second World has passed from the scene, this internal critique in the First World must ally itself with the protest of those who suffer in the Third World in order finally to introduce justice into the global economic system. But where are the alternatives and the utopias?

(1) The cold war is over, the centralized socialism of Eastern Europe has disappeared, and no one in Europe can even discuss Marxism anymore. Michael Gorbachev's suggestion to build a "common house for Europe" contains colossal new opportunities, both good and evil. The European Union will grow, and Western and Eastern European countries will unite in a democratic confederation. The problems lie in the imbalance in the standard of living between West and East: How can equal conditions be created in the wealthy West and the poor East Germany? The German and European unification will have to be realized in the face of the stream of persons moving from the East to the West. Without social justice there will be no peace in Europe. It is true that the common free market encourages personal initiative, but it also leaves in its wake social disparities. The future tasks of the churches and of political theology lie precisely at this point: on behalf of the victims of market economy systems—not in the name of an ideology—to stand publicly for the critique of capitalism and to create justice for people and nature through social and environmental politics. True, this is not convenient at the moment, but Catholic social teaching since *Rerum Novarum* (1891) contains a great deal of potential for doing it. This is no less true of the power of religious-social movements in Protestant Christianity.

We are not familiar in our churches and congregations with any "base community" movement worth mentioning, but for 150 years our churches have been deeply engaged in diaconal service. The largest portion of social diaconal service to children, the disabled, sick, and elderly has been placed in the hands of the churches of our country. This Christian diaconal service to the victims of the free market economy of our society would be misused if it were not to be connected to a prophetic critique of the perpetrators and the system that produces these victims. With the passing of the so-called communist threat, I see the rise of necessary internal conflicts between church and state and between Christianity and society taking its place.

(2) No less significant is the ecological conflict with nature into which industrial society has gotten itself. In this connection private and public consciousness of environmental issues has greatly increased in the last ten years and calls for changes in production and consumption. Ecological theology here sides with God's misused and devastated creation, which we sacrifice as we continue to live at its expense, and it protects against the perpetrators and the system that produce such victims. Ecological theology, too, is Christian diaconal service to suffering nature and prophetic critique of the violence that produces this suffering.

(3) Political theology in Europe was from the beginning ecumenical in spirit and developed in the context of international relations with Latin America, Korea, and Africa. But the rise of a new Europe is accompanied by a new Eurocentrism among Europeans, which the Christian churches must resist in the name of their worldwide catholicity. Christians in Europe must become advocates for those outside. Nationalism is growing in Europe at the moment. We need ecumenical solidarity that can become stronger than loyalty to one's nation or to Europe! This is not only a moral obligation but the only course that makes sense as well. Without social justice between the First and Third Worlds, there is no peace. Without peace with the Third World, the world of the North Atlantic will destroy itself. The ecological consequences of the misery in the Third World are already having repercussions in the First World. A humanity divided by violence and injustice will destroy the *one earth* upon which we all live.

Political theology is *internal critique* of the modern world. Liberation theology is *external critique* of the modern world. Both speak in the name of the victims. Must there not be an alliance between critical theology in the First World and liberation theology in the Third?

The Future of Liberation Theology

Thus far only the Latinos have spoken in the new Latin American theology.[15] When will the black descendants of the slaves in Brazil and indigenous women raise their voices? And when the Indians raise themselves, will they still speak in the categories of a Christian theology, or will they separate themselves from the Christianity into which they were violently coerced and return to their former cultures and religions?[16] The blacks in Brazil and the Caribbean could also find their old African Macumba cults more attractive than Christianity even if it were represented by some form of liberation theology.

When in the future Latin America, too, ceases to be a purely "Christian continent," will not Latin American liberation theology have to expand its boundaries to include interreligious dialogue? An interreligious dialogue from the perspective of liberation theology would be something new in these conversations which have thus far served more the cause of peaceful co-existence among the various religious communities—"No world peace without peace among religions" (Hans Küng)—than they have the common struggle against oppression and for the liberation of the people. This expansion already became clear when the attempt was made to transfer Latin American theology of liberation to the Asian context, and it became evident that the masses of Asia's poor are not Christians, and Christian theology did not have much to offer them. If liberation theology is to be expanded in this way, however, it will mean expanding itself in its fundamentals. Thus far it has focused on the conflicts between poor and rich, oppression and liberation, almost exclusively in socioeconomic terms, and has paid insufficient attention to the cultural and religious dimensions of the conflict in a given country and among a given people. When I carefully urged this in my "open letter" to José Míguez Bonino, it was still indignantly rejected. The fact that today in Latin and South America more and more people are turning to new religious movements such as the Afro-Brazilian cults, and that the Christian Pentecostal movement is attracting the masses, is related to this deficit in early liberation theology. The poor want to be addressed not only in terms of what they do not have, but to also be respected for who they are.

For a long time worry about the destruction of the rain forest in Latin America was regarded as typical for the First World. For the poor landless farmers of Brazil economic worry concerning daily survival is the primary reality. It is only in recent years that the realization has penetrated Latin American liberation theology that economics and ecology belong inseparably together and that it is suicidal to consume the basis for one's own existence.

Following the emergence in the mid-70s in Europe, especially in overindustrialized Germany, of an ecological-political theology along the lines of the North American model (John Cobb, Harvey Cox, and others), an ecological liberation theology is now also beginning to develop (D.E.I. in Costa Rica, Leonardo Boff, Reinerio Arce Valentin in Cuba) and allying itself with the early beginnings of an ecological politics in Brazil. Of theological interest is Leonardo Boff's vision of a new planetary bio-ethos which fits very well into the new "theology of life."[17] It introduces a new perspective into our ecological discourse. In terms of liberation theology, the issue is not only "the preservation of the creation," as the conciliar proceedings say, but the liberation of nature from human oppression and the reintegration of human culture into the living organism of the earth. It was in the service of this vision that Ernesto Cardenal composed his mighty and beautiful "Cantico Cosmico."[18]

The feminist movement in North America, "Women's Liberation," developed parallel to the Civil Rights Movement. Feminist theology began as an endeavor in theology as such but very quickly adopted its methods from liberation theology. In the U.S. and Europe feminist theologians understood themselves as liberation theologians, and in Latin America in the last ten years a remarkable indigenous form of liberation theology has emerged. *Mujerista* theology corresponds to black womanist theology (e.g., Delores Williams) in distinguishing itself from white middle-class theology. The category "poor" homogenized what in fact can be clearly differentiated, namely women as subjects of economic exploitation, social disenfranchisement, and cultural humiliation caused by *machismo*. They are victims not only of economic and political but also sexual violence. In addition to the critique of patriarchal images of God, which one finds in the U.S. and Europe as well, Latin American women have assumed leading roles in the Christian base communities and thus called into question the male priestly caste. In Elsa Tamez the Protestant Seminario Biblico Latinomericana in San José, Costa Rica, now has its first female rector.

The most sensitive point in liberation theology as a whole, however, lies not outside but within itself. Without a liberated church no liberated society, without church reform no social revolution! Since the famous Latin American Bishops' Conferences in Medellín in 1968 and Puebla in 1979 there has been the hope that the episcopate and theology would together bring to realization the ecclesial "option for the poor," that the church of Latin America as the "church of the poor" and the "church of the people" would initiate a universal reformation of the Roman Catholic church, and that in similar fashion liberation theology would assume a leading position in the global class struggle (George Casalis). These hopes were shattered by Rome and Vatican politics. Of course, one can quote the Pope's words: "The theology of liberation is not only opportune, but useful and necessary."[19] It is better, however, to pay attention to the Pope's deeds. The bishops named since Puebla have made the adherents of liberation theology in the Latin American episcopate a minority. Cardinal Arns and Cardinal Lorscheider were severely limited in their effectiveness. In the chair of the martyr Archbishop Oscar Arnulfo Romero now sits an Opus Dei man. It depresses one deeply to mention that John Paul II, on the occasion of General Augusto Pinochet's golden wedding anniversary, sent a golden gift with a personal greeting to the murderer of so many Christians in Chile. Certainly one can mention the two documents from the Congregation for the Faith in which Cardinal Ratzinger finally arrived at a balanced assessment of the theology of liberation. But it is better to pay attention to his deeds and listen to the long passion narrative story of Leonardo Boff, who was coerced into giving up the priestly office and leaving the Franciscan order and who, in departing, wrote bitterly: "The doctrinaire power is cruel and merciless."[20] Were Medellín and Puebla church dreams in which the liberation theologians placed too much trust? Have they struggled too little for freedom in the church, as Hans Küng has accused them? Of course there is the church of the base communities and in many countries one has the impression that there are two Catholic churches existing side by side: here the base communities, there the hierarchy. In any case, it is clear that one cannot build a new, just, and free society with an old, feudalistic, authoritarian church. "We are the people" applies to politics *and* church or it does not apply at all. As long as the feudalistic-authoritarian, hierarchical structure of the colonial church in Latin America remains intact, it will function as a model for a corresponding class society. Many of those who wish to experience the church as "the people of God," as the Second Vatican Council declared, and as the living community of Christ, and who hold fast to the hope for a "church of the people" in the tradition of Medellín and Puebla, will join the congregations of the Protestant Pentecostal movement, which are still scornfully designated as "sects" by church administrators. Here, it seems to me, is the most difficult but most important challenge confronting the theology of liberation: the liberation of the church itself from the holy reign to be the community of the people.

The Theology of Our Liberation

The Globalization of the Third World

The facts are not hard to recognize: the present globalization of business, the relocation of production sites to so-called cheap-wage countries, and the opening of global markets not only bring our industry into the Third World, but also brings the Third World to us. We ourselves are becoming the Third World. The concept was originally intended to be not only geographical but social as well and to refer to the poor lower classes of society. So we experience the Third World in our midst. The U.N. report "On Human Development" (1996) calls attention to the dangers of making more people poor in order to make a few people even wealthier. The wealth of 358 billionaires exceeds the total income of the poor countries in which nearly 45 percent of the human race lives! "If present trends continue, the economic disparity between industrialized nations and developing nations will assume proportions which are no longer merely unjust, but inhuman," declared J.C. Speth, General Secretary of the UN Development programs.[21]

But this injustice and inhumanity are increasing in the industrialized nations themselves. This year more than 100 million people in North America, Europe, Japan and Australia are living below the official poverty line, nearly 30 million of them homeless. The numbers from Germany are also alarming: 7.5 million poor people, 900,000 homeless. An effective social policy to counter this development is not in sight. What seems to be visible instead is a capitulation on the part of politicians in the face of the "realities" of the economic system which globalization favors with greater profits and fewer taxes. Those thrust into poverty continue to survive in our country on the very edge of minimal requirements for existence, whereas in the underdeveloped nations—according to a UN report—25,000 children die each day from hunger or from diseases which have long been curable.[22]

Apparently the globalization of business leads in our own societies not to *solidarity* but to *disassociation*, a fact proven by the continual complaints that costs for social services are too high. Insurance companies attempt to force the aged and the chronically ill out. Dialysis is no longer available to persons over 60 years old in England unless they pay for the treatment themselves. When a person is only measured by her or his market value, and their human dignity is ignored, then a child with a long life expectancy may be valued at 1.5 million dollars while a retiree is worthless since he or she can no longer produce for society. As a result, it is not easy to brush aside the fear that the disabled, the old, and useless in our society must fear for their lives. Even nations of the so-called First World end up in conditions of apartheid. Poverty in the family and hopelessness among the young people living with them bring an increase in crime, in response to which the wealthy and the "better paid" live in "gated communities," in secure areas, while other housing deteriorates into slums, as is currently happening in South Africa. When a strong middle class disintegrates, political democracy is finished as well, because the democratic ideal of equality is irreconcilable with an economic system that produces increasing inequality.

The clearer this development becomes to those of us in the nations of the First World, the more we ourselves discover the oppressed, impoverished, and abandoned world in our midst, the more relevant Latin American liberation theology becomes for us. It would be better to pay attention to its basic insights now than to await the tragic end of capitalism which will not have been destroyed by its socialist alternative, as it turns out no real alternative at all, but was rather condemned to fail because of its constantly increasing violations against human dignity, against life on this earth, and against its own future.

On the Way to a Common Theology of Life

If it is correct to say that the globalization of production sites and markets has brought the unjust and inhuman conditions of the Third World into the nations of the (geographic) First World, then the relevance of Third World liberation theology becomes universal. Latin American theology of liberation is the first theological alternative to capitalism, "the global marketing of everything" as it is known today. It is contextual theology, not just for Latin America, but universally so, in the wake of the developments I have described. It speaks on behalf of the impoverished and excluded in Los Angeles and Bangkok, in England and Romania, in East Germany and in South Africa, to mention only a few regions. Thus it is taken up by others and transferred into their situation. In this way it will also be transformed from a specifically Latin American to a universal social-critical theology. *Third World* is a class concept. In this way the theology of liberation moves beyond its Roman Catholic boundaries and becomes catholic in a wider ecumenical sense. It will move beyond the boundaries of a Christian religious community in order to nurture every impulse toward human liberation from injustice and oppression that comes from the common people. Latin America may still be seen as a "Christian continent," not so Asia and Africa. The mission of liberation theology is as universal as human suffering.

For the European context it seems to me that an important starting point is to place the liberation theology of the poor in the wider horizon of the reign of God because this allows us to name the positive good that is to be achieved by means of the liberation from oppression and poverty. This positive element remains connected to the negative that is to be overcome, however, for Jesus brought the reign of God to the poor, not to the rich. But since the time of Constantine, theology of the reign of God has been connected with Christian kingdoms or Christian civilization. Therefore, theology centering on the reign of God can only be pursued if it is inseparably linked to the Beatitudes of the Sermon on the Mount and Jesus' call to discipleship. Otherwise such theology has nothing to do with Christ. But what is the meaning of "reign of God?" Jon Sobrino speaks to the point: "The reign of God is life, life in its fullness and the fulfillment of life." We can, then, fill liberation theology's reign of God theology with "life." Structural and personal acts of violence against life characterize our world to a terrifying degree: violence against human beings, violence against earth's nature, violence against the future of life. The love of life and reverence for life must be reawakened in order to combat the growing cynicism in the First World. Means of protecting the life of the weak, the life of all fellow creatures, and the future of our common life must be developed to confront the violent structures of death.

Liberation from violence and poverty remains the theme of every practical theology and every theological praxis. Alongside freedom, however, we have the other theme that has been nearly forgotten and greatly repressed since the demise of the socialist world: *equality*. Without equality there is no such thing as a free world. We speak out of the spirit of primitive Christianity when we hold this truth to be self-evident, "that every human being is created *free and equal*." Equality does not refer to some form of collectivism but rather to equal conditions and possibilities of life for every person. As a social concept equality means *justice*. As a humanitarian concept equality means *solidarity*. As a Christian concept equality means *love*. Either we will create a world of social justice, human solidarity, and Christian love, or this world will perish because of human oppression at the hands of other human beings, because of antisocial egotism, and because of the destruction of the future for the sake of short-term benefits. Either social justice or growing criminality and ever more expensive security systems. Either international justice or revolts of starving people in poor countries. Either decision today for long-term investment in the future of a life together or short-term profits today and calculated bankruptcy for humankind in the near future.

Latin American theology of liberation could awaken in Europe a new social theology of the reign of God tracing itself back to the more left-oriented forms of Catholic social teaching, back to the religious-social movements of Leonhard Ragaz, Eduard Heimann, Paul Tillich, and the young Karl Barth, and pulling together the various beginnings made by political theology, ecological theology, feminist theology, and the social-critical theology. Not least, even Pope John Paul II could associate himself with such a theological enterprise since it would fulfill his dream of a "culture of life."

Translated by Virgil Howard

GAYRAUD S. WILMORE

6. Black Consciousness
Stumbling Block
or Battering Ram?

Black theologians, no less than white, worry about the corrosive effects of extreme pluralism upon the theological fidelity of the church. Indeed, part of the impetus of black theology was in response to the allegation that there was no theology worth the name in the black church and that the low level of biblical and doctrinal understanding in the mainstream black denominations was deplorable. I would venture to say, nevertheless, that we have been more willing to entertain the redemptive possibilities in culture—particularly in an African American culture infused with black spirituality and militant church action for justice—than are many of our colleagues on the other side of the color line. This more positive, hopeful view of culture that is found in James H. Cone, J. Deotis Roberts, Diana L. Hayes, Dwight N. Hopkins, Jacquelyn Grant, and younger black theologians, stems from a disinclination to erect too thick a partition between the black church and the black community. These theologians do not sacralize black culture—particularly in view of today's attenuation of an authentic African inheritance and the trivialization of black urban culture by the hucksters of gangsta rap and hip-hop who get rich exploiting black youth—but they do perceive a spiritual bond between poor and disprivileged African Americans and the religious institutions that first gave them the soul-force to resist dehumanization.

Black and White Theology

The primary carriers of black culture have always been ordinary church folk—especially church women, the poets and novelists, the artists and musicians, and the street people who joined them in support of religious leaders like Henry M. Turner, Adam Clayton Powell Jr., Malcolm X, Martin Luther King Jr., and Jesse Jackson.

The question that concerned Frederick Herzog, Edward Huenemannn, Ben Reist, Peter C. Hodgson, and several other white friends of the black church movement[1] was whether black theologians were stretching their radicalism beyond the pale of interracial coalition-building and cross-cultural theological collaboration by emphasizing blackness rather than social justice. They wanted to know, in other words, if the "ethnic specificity" of black and womanist theologies turned out to be only an expression of an outmoded religiocultural tribalism. They feared that the historic unity of the church across racial and ethnic boundaries was being sacrificed to an ambiguous emphasis upon a blackness for which no white person could be expected to qualify. The very fact that the Society for the Study of Black Religion, organized in 1970, never opened its doors to white scholars may have given some credence to the suspicion that black theology had been seduced by tribalism.

A few members of the Society never agreed that white scholars, if admitted to the S.S.B.R., would inevitably reshape its mission and finally take it over. Although I thought that fear was exaggerated, I did, nevertheless, understand the uneasiness that some of my colleagues felt about interracial organizations. All of us wanted to be sure, to the extent possible, that white scholars like Paul Lehmann and Frederick Herzog, who had publicly recognized the value of the work we were doing, were sincerely committed to lifting up the distinctive contributions of African and African American religion and culture and not simply interested in buttressing their own political position vis-á-vis the white religious establishment.[2]

It was not easy then and is not easy today for white theologians to rid themselves of the notion that we live in a color-blind society, or one that has reached a point where it ought to be blind to color and ethnicity. The failure among some white scholars to concede that racial prejudice in the United States, if not in the whole Western world, still impedes the general valorization of black life and culture as well as the distribution of justice to all, is partly related to their illusions about what the Civil Rights Movement actually accomplished—as documented by what they read in *Ebony* and *Jet*, and the deceptive images of racial integration they see on prime-time television. The other part may be their inability to face up to the racism in themselves, hidden in denial. The aplomb with which many white academics and church bureaucrats seem to regard Proposition 209 in California and the negative mood of the courts about correcting disabilities still conjoined with growing up black in the United States, indicates where some of our former friends in the academy and the church have gone. Alas, they have gone back to the cold, cold world which believes that to continue to fight racism only coddles the black poor, divides society into warring camps, and ultimately does more harm than good.

The Meaning of Blackness

White theologians and scholars in religion who were born and raised in the United States should know better than they do about the symbolic meaning of blackness in the consciousness of both white and black Americans. The shame is that few of them have given enough attention and study, or have had enough genuine experience in the African American community, to really understand the psychosomatic depths that are plumbed and stirred up by the idea of blackness, by the profound symbolic meaning of the word in our living vocabularies.

When I was a boy growing up in the Negro ghetto of North Philadelphia during the Great Depression, there was a "toast" or folk saying among us that I remember now with both bitterness over its inevitability and astonishment over its visualization of the state of black being. I don't know where it came from originally, but it seems clear that it was somehow related to Psalm 90 and was part of the street ritual of our socialization to both the black church and the harsh realities of black existence in the nation of our birth.

> *Dark man, born of a dark woman*
> *sees dark days;*
> *Rises up in the morning like a*
> *hopper-grass,*

> *Cut down in the evening like*
> *asparagras.*

The oral tradition contains other sayings like this that were a part of the folklore of the post-World War I era in our communities—the street pedagogy of the black oppressed. I particularly remember these two, which reveal the same sentiment of self-degradation and forsakenness:

> *Oh, Lord, will I ever, will I ever?*
> *No nigger, never! Never!*
> *Well, where there's life there's hope.*
> *Yes, and where there's a tree*
> *there's a rope.*
>
> * * *
>
> *If you're white, you're right;*
> *If yellow, you're mellow;*
> *If you're brown, stick around;*
> *But if you're black, step back.*

There was another side of blackness, expressed in sayings like "the blacker the berry the sweeter the juice," but these more self-esteeming proverbs were rarer and did not prevent most of us from wanting to fight anyone who had the nerve to call us black. Young African Americans living today cannot possibly imagine the force of the cultural revolution that, like a raging flood bursting through an obsolescent dam, swept over their parents and grandparents when black became beautiful and blackness a metaphor for humanization and liberation. It was the period of the 1960s and 70s that brought about the transition from Negro to black. The growing alienation of the Student Nonviolent Coordinating Committee from the Southern Christian Leadership Conference after the Meredith Freedom March in June 1966; the summer rebellions in scores of cities that are cited in the Kerner Commission's report on civil disorder; and the rise of the Black Power movement, the National Committee of Black Churchmen, and the widespread demand for black studies in American colleges and universities—all mark a historic change in the consciousness of African Americans that has by no means run its full course on the eve of the twenty-first century. As always, for good or ill, as goes the black community goes the black church. C. Eric Lincoln saw clearly why the Negro church had to become the black church and the depth of the revolution that King had started but did not live long enough to see its second stage:

> The Negro Church is dead because the norms and presuppositions which structured and conditioned it are not relevant norms and presuppositions. . . . The Black Church is or must become the characteristic expression of institutionalized religion for contemporary Blackamericans because it is the perfect counterpart of the Black [person's] present self-perception and the way he sees God and man, particularly the white man, in a new structuring of relationships. . . . [3]

This "new structuring of relationships" required a new theology that perceived the hand of God in the conscientization of the black masses for political action by the revalorization of blackness as a symbol of personal and collective liberation. Thus, for all the problems and ambiguities that accompanied a change that many white people regarded as superficial, blackness and whiteness as color terms became critically important for the way many African American Christians think theologically. Most white European and American theologians and ordinary white church members were baffled by the implications of this "obsession with color" that they presumed the black theology movement to be about. Even Latin American liberation theologians were vaguely uncomfortable with the language of color symbolism and felt that it mistakenly wrapped the gospel in a cultural husk that, as well-meaning and justified as it might be, obscured the universal and political requirements of a liberation praxis.

To accuse African Americans of being obsessed with color is like accusing fish of being obsessed with water or human beings of being obsessed with fresh air and sunlight. Where one's environment has been saturated for centuries with the demonstrable substantiality of color, to be concerned with how to live and move in such an environment, what to do with it, how to make it work for health and life rather than for sickness unto death, is not so much to be obsessed with it as to be forced to come to terms with it as sensible, responsible human beings. Anyone who has not grown up in a culture in which color symbolism is deeply etched into the fabric of his or her life and consciousness will be unable to understand the full import of blackness and whiteness in the experience of being human in America. Blackness and whiteness are so deeply rooted in what it means to be an American that they have become in the United States, consciously and unconsciously, sources and norms for thinking theologically and ordering the life and work of the Christian churches.

The Apostle Paul reminds us that, having passed through earthen vessels, the treasure of Christian revelation is never delivered from heaven pure and unalloyed (2 Cor. 4:7). For African Americans it is just as natural to speak of a black theology as of a German theology, or a Japanese theology, or a Latin American liberation theology. It has not always been so for us, but in the last thirty years—since the revolution—we have been more conscious of being, in some senses, a nation within a nation. All of these contextual theologies have to do with a collective identity, a sense of peoplehood, a matter of time, place, language, and custom through which the Christian gospel has always been filtered as it makes its way from the throne of God to the hearts and minds of believers.

Religion and Color Symbolism

The color symbolism that permeates the consciousness of the African American antedates the Atlantic slave trade and colonialism. It goes back at least as early as the rabbinical formulation of the so-called Hamitic hypothesis regarding the origin of the black peoples of the earth as interpreted by the Babylonian Talmud of the sixth century C.E.[4] During the medieval period black color and physiognomy were widely believed to be the dire consequence of Noah's curse of the Hamitic progeny in Genesis 9:25-27.[5] The ancient myth about the origin of the races and that the black race was cursed not only by Noah but by God played an important role in the attitude whites had toward blacks in New England under the Puritans and in the South before and after the Civil War. But the argument of some Christian scholars that the Euroamerican mind did not succumb to racism properly understood until modern times seems like an academic conceit that will not stand up to relentless scrutiny.

I cannot believe that there were no negative psychological reactions among the African Christians during the first four centuries of the Christian era when they were consoled by their white brothers and sisters that "though you may be black on the outside, you are white on the inside by the blood of Christ," or that they were unaware of some sneakily ambiguous connotation in the petition to God to "wash us that we may be whiter than snow." No matter how much some whites continue to protest that there was no invidious color-consciousness attached to these sayings that we find in the literature of the early church, I cannot help but believe that we have here a hint of a basically pathetic and flawed self-image that was imposed on blacks, a sense of an imputed color pollution and deprivation of whiteness. If the Bible itself seems to equate whiteness with purity, some African Christians must have felt that there had to be something unaccountably wrong with being black—even on the outside. If the Hamitic hypothesis did not offer an acceptable explanation, it at least suggested to Christians of both colors that it was no mere accident of nature that Europeans were born of one color and Africans and Asians of another. Some preternatural design must have been at work. The question must have occurred in the contact between black African and European Christians, "If one had a color preference, which would one prefer?"

The pejorative connotation continued in the English language where we speak of "blackmail," "blackguards," "black sheep of the family," or having one's reputation "blackened." All of these, and many more that we can find in the dictionaries, are negative images. On the other hand, whiteness has consistently been presented as positive—connoting goodness, cleanliness, beauty, and purity. It would be much fairer to make the case that we are *all* somehow "obsessed" with color, for as much as we may deplore it, the color symbolism of our language in Great Britain and North America gives the whiteness/blackness dichotomy almost ontological significance—at least up to the end of the twentieth century.

Unless the next century brings some change that we cannot foresee, almost all the visual media in the United States will continue to remind us of the degradation of dark skin color—books, newspapers, magazines, billboards, movies, and television. Even though the employment of black newscasters, actors and actresses, fashion models, beauty contestants, and talk-show hosts and hostesses has reduced the impression of the debasement of an earlier period, it is still true that many children grow up in our society with the feeling that they are lacking something critically important for happiness and success in life if they are not white or, at least, of a light skin color. Many of us, both black and white, have tried to evade the embarrassment of the situation, but even the pictures of Christ hanging on the walls of our Sunday School rooms suggest the superiority of white skin color, for this Lord, whom we are called to imitate and follow in all respects, is presented to the world as a white man. Since the revolution of the 1960s more and more black children cannot help but ask the question of themselves, if not of their teachers, "If he is indeed white, with blond hair and blue eyes, and I am black, with kinky hair and brown eyes, I wonder what this Christ has really to do with me."

In our country, therefore, there continues to be this nagging feeling of something being wrong, of some kind of deprivation, of inferiority and unworthiness related to color. There is among many African Americans a sense of indelible infection that one can only be rid of if God will "wash me and make me whiter than snow." Since nothing changes on the outside, there is even reason for doubt and cynicism about what can happen on the inside.

I recall that once during my teen years I got into a fight with a white boy on the Benjamin Franklin Parkway in my hometown of Philadelphia. It started when I accidentally bumped into him in a crowd of mostly white people who were massed on the sidewalk to watch a patriotic parade moving along the Parkway. He yelled at me, backing away, "Stay away from me, you black nigger! Now I gotta go home and wash to get your black offa me!" I realized then, I think for the first time, that my color was an offense to white people. I had known for a long time that there was something not quite right about me, that I was being treated differently in elementary school and in public places, but that jolting experience on the Parkway made it clear why—it was my color! My dark skin color was the thing that whites feared and rejected because it was believed somehow to stain, to contaminate, to make impure.

That early revelation was, of course, soon reinforced by the explanations black parents and teachers gave for our being discriminated against in many areas of life. I don't recall that it was particularly agonizing to hear those explanations—perhaps because we lived in a more or less isolated black world, even in the North, and as children our contacts with whites were relatively infrequent. But I do remember what it was like to have to explain color prejudice after I myself became a parent. If one has never been a black parent, one cannot appreciate the agony of having to tell a child that he or she cannot do this or that, or go here or there because he or she is black. Blackness, whether we like it or not, has been a mark of oppression in the United States, and although the situation has changed since my boyhood, the color of one's skin continues to affect one's daily existence in myriad ways. W. E. B. DuBois never spoke more correctly than when he declared that the problem of the twentieth century would be the color line. I am tempted to enumerate the instances of racial prejudice and discrimination that are being talked about and investigated even as I write, but let it suffice to say that one can scarcely open a newspaper or magazine published in the African American community (don't expect an accurate picture of what is going on from the white media) without reading about acts of racial violence that seem to ebb and flow in our nation.

What is this all about? What is it about the white man of the West that makes him hate blackness with such a passion that sometimes he seems to wish that it were abolished from the earth? Other races can be assimilated. Even immigrants from other nonwhite nations are readily received in our country today and become honorary members of the majority society. But for too many older white Americans, and for many who are still young, the blackness that is associated with African Americans who were born and raised in this society is utterly adversative, something that must be blotted out of existence as if it were an affront to God. There is no question but that such an attitude sooner or later incites to violence and genocide. How these deep-lying feelings can exist alongside of the sexual adulation of the sensuous black female body, the celebration of sports figures, the hysterical acclaim of singers like Michael Jackson, and the enormous popularity of celebrities like Oprah Winfrey, is a mystery that continues to baffle us. Some people have theorized about the deep psychological source of this madness—alluding to our ancient, archetypal preference for the lightness of the daylight sky and the fear and antipathy toward the darkness of the night which held terrors unthinkable for primitive humans. I have no explanation for either the fact or the exceptions. I only know that color prejudice and racism are endemic in American society and we should not, for the sake of being polite to one another, give up the right and duty to speak about them, to struggle to understand them, and to oppose them with all our might.

Where We Are Now

Since the first African was disembarked on the quays of the New World, religion has been one of the major forms of opposition that black people have chosen. It devolved upon highly trained African American church men and women of the last half of the twentieth century to uncover a rich and deep-lying vein of resistance in the quarry of black belief and folklore. Out of this source black Christians have hewn a monument of black theological criticism. In the face of ridicule and rejection from the white academy, professional theologians like Cone and Roberts hammered out the main outlines of a black liberation theology, which drew its wisdom and emotive power not only from the Old and New Testaments but from the living traditions of African American culture.

It was important in those early, formative years of the 1960s to listen to the left wing of the Civil Rights Movement and later to grassroots leaders of the Black Power movement. We had, first of all, to do something about the way black people thought of themselves and the way they understood the meaning of their experience in this country in the light of the revelation of Jesus Christ. It was not so much a matter of creating a theology as it was of retrieving one that had been concealed beneath a patina of white evangelicalism. Before the Civil War black Christian writers and thinkers had already rejected the spiritualization of the message of the New Testament by the mainstream white churches which robbed it of all political salience. Then came the missionary inundation of the South during Reconstruction by the white churches of the North, the rise of an apolitical Holiness and Pentecostalism, the influence of urban revivalism under the Dwight L. Moodys and Billy Sundays, and later under Billy Graham. These developments on the American religious front served to blunt the radicalism which characterized the black church during the twenty years leading up to the Civil War. But there were, by the turn of the century, the implications of the Social Gospel for many black urban churches, and even more importantly, there were powerful resources in black culture that helped the new theologians reinterpret the message of Jesus Christ in terms of the struggle for justice and liberation for black and other oppressed people. The remarkable ministry of Martin Luther King Jr. laid the foundation for the work of the National

Committee of Black Churchmen and the black caucuses of the major white denominations, which opened up the floodgates of cultural and theological self-esteem and anti-racism. Many in the black community, if not immediately in the churches, believed that it was necessary to reverse the color symbolism of white Western civilization—turning it on its head, as it were—in order to rid black folk of the self-abnegation and feeling of powerlessness that white Christianity had, wittingly and unwittingly, fostered for generations.

By now many of us have gone through a process in which we first experienced a paralyzing, secret feeling of inferiority; second, a profound hatred of white people and everything that is white; third, an exaggeration of the intrinsic worth of blackness, sometimes expressed in such phrases as "Black is beautiful" and "blacker than thou"; and finally a stage in which we came to a realistic acceptance of self and others, a candid appraisal and theological understanding of who we are and how we came to be this way. With this transition from Negro to black came also an ability to look unblinkingly at white people for who they were and an appreciation of them when they strove to be what God created them to be. This final stage is not yet complete in any of us. It is ongoing into the future. But for these closing years of the twentieth century it is the black community's best chance for true liberation and reconciliation in a multicultural America.

Reconciliation Prematurely?

The problem with some of our white friends, and Frederick Herzog may have been among them during the 1980s, is that they wanted us to move more rapidly, and I would say, prematurely, through these stages toward the ultimate goal of racial reconciliation. They wanted to see us do theology *beyond* black consciousness. Some of us believe, notwithstanding Victor Anderson's provocative demurrer,[6] that one must go through blackness in order to get beyond it, and that even beyond it one will still feel its gravitational pull until the god of racism has been dethroned in America. In other words, we must somehow confront and reconstruct the symbolism by which we have been wounded in order to be healed and become capable of healing others. In some way that black theologians have not yet made entirely clear, it is at this point that the suffering and victory of Jesus

Christ become meaningful for the contemporary African American Christian; a point at which she or he is able to speak boldly and truthfully of "the Black Messiah."

There is no need for an apology, even if this may sound like one. We have, I think, made it quite clear that blackness has to do with more than skin color. The symbol partakes of the reality it partially conceals and partially discloses, but it is not that reality in any totalistic sense. We cannot entirely expunge the relationship the symbol bears to our experience of being of a negative color in America, but it has to do with more than the color of our skin. Blackness can symbolize for both blacks and all others both oppression and the suffering and struggle necessary to transcend it. The fundamental theological meaning of blackness is its appropriate representation of what Jesus suffered and, through the resurrection, ultimately overcame as the Oppressed Man of God who sits at the right hand of God and will come again to judge the earth.

One of the most powerful expressions of this connection between blackness and Jesus as the Oppressed Man of God is found in a poem written by the South African theologian Gabriel M. Setiloane. Only a few verses can be quoted here:

A wee little babe wrapped in swaddling clothes.
Ah, if only He had been like little Moses, lying
Sun-scorched on the banks of the River of God
We would have recognized Him.
He eludes us still this Jesus, Son of Man.

His words, Ah, they taste so good
As sweet and refreshing as the sap of the palm
raised and nourished on African soil
The Truths of His words are for all men, for all time.

And yet for us it is when He is on the cross,
This Jesus of Nazareth, with holed hands
and open side, like a beast at a sacrifice:
When He is stripped naked like us,
Browned and sweating water and blood in the heat of the sun,
Yet silent,
That we cannot resist Him.

How like us He is, this Jesus of Nazareth,
Beaten, tortured, imprisoned, spat upon, truncheoned,

Denied by His own, and chased like a thief in the night.
Despised, and rejected like a dog that has fleas,
For NO REASON.[7]

When our slave ancestors sang, "Were you there when they crucified my Lord?" the answer was in their hearts if not on their lips. "Yes, we were there when they hung that poor nigger on the cross. We were there because we were with him. We are like him and he is like us!" Perhaps not all people can put the matter in that way, but all oppressed people can appropriate the spiritual meaning and power of that declaration—"Yes, we were there!" Blackness should be understood in the sense of weakness, degradation, and rejection through that dark experience whose mystery has not yet been pierced, also understood in the sense of strength in struggle, salvation from trouble, resurrection from death, and exaltation in the world to come.

African American Christians, therefore, are not ready to surrender this rich symbol, which carries all the mystery and illumination of our historical sojourn and vocation. Since it was not created by our theologians but came up out of the life of our people, we will continue to try to understand it, to wrestle with it, to make it useful for the humanization, mobilization, and liberation of all people who want to be free, who want to be at some different place than where they are now in the world that somebody else imposed upon them.

That such a transfiguration is necessary in this country is too obvious to argue about. Look at the Senate of the United States, at the court system, at the assemblies of the intellectual elite of the nation, into the board rooms and executive suites of corporate America. What do you see? Turn on C-Span and other public affairs programs on your television set. How often do you see blacks on the distinguished panels, at the head tables, or even in the audiences in that rarefied atmosphere at the summit of the scientific, economic, political, and international affairs totem poles of the world? More, indeed, than fifty years ago, but still not enough. Still not as often as on the basketball court, the football field, or the music videos. Why is this so? Why are most of the people who live on the top floors of this world-house white American or white European males—though in recent years one must acknowledge an increasing number of white females?

Who built this house? Did God? Decidedly not, and here we have no need for inclusive language. *Men* built this house! Mainly white men built it over a thousand years ago, then renovated it after the Industrial Revolution, then repaired it after the First World War, and today are desperately maintaining and defending it. Its weight-bearing pillars and superstructure, fashioned over many centuries, are held intact by white power, and that power makes it almost impossible for millions of others to have access to the upper floors. If you will bear with the metaphor a moment longer—stairs suddenly run out; doors that should open into hallways open instead into airless closets; intricate passageways lead from one level to another. But if you live where most of us live in this house you cannot find those passageways, or you discover them blocked! Glass ceilings and mirrored partitions abound and create the illusion of access or egress that simply do not exist.

Down deep in the basement of this world-house generation after generation of the occupants live and die in rooms that resemble prison cells. They have little space for growth, maneuver, or elevation to upper levels. So in the bowels of this house a sometimes noisy but mostly quiet and desperate rebellion is going on. It never sleeps. It is perennial. Its aim is to tear down those walls, shatter those fake ceilings, and break through those locked doors and blocked staircases in the name of the justice that Fred Herzog wrote so eloquently about. Jesus said that in God's mansion there were many rooms, but Herzog knew that the Lord was not referring to anything like this house we live in today.

The theology of blackness is the critical thinking and praxis designed to dismantle this house in order to build something more like what Jesus was talking about. But it is a theology that cannot be foreshortened or prematurely universalized. It is a thinking and praxis that must draw its essential sustenance and energy from a specific culture that was fused long ago out of the bits and pieces found in that special corner of the basement where black people have languished. That is what the second generation of black, Afrocentric, and womanist theologians, like Delores S. Williams, Cain Hope Felder, Dwight N. Hopkins, Forest Harris, Jacquelyn Grant, and Diana L. Hayes, are trying to draw from when they research African Traditional Religions, the slave narratives, the spirituals and the blues, or explore the impertinence and toughness of black mamas who not only have stopped working in Miss Daisy's kitchen, but wouldn't be caught driving her through Atlanta's Piedmont Park.

Of course, we still do not know how these younger black thinkers can use this basement culture of blackness without being seduced by it. The United Church of Christ document on "Sound Teaching" which Herzog had a large hand in shaping, is helpful when it declares, "The church can be engaged with culture without being co-opted by culture as court chaplain . . . the church is people working for an obedient culture in keeping with God's will—an unending task."[8]

Today some liberal Protestants who are engaged in that unending task are exploring the possibility of a pluralistic culture that wipes out invidious distinctions while still being obedient to the will of God. Albeit, some of us still believe that we cannot effectively contribute to that multiform culture without first shoring up our own consciousness and self-understandings. That may not be true for other groups coming to America these days, but the future of the black church, and perhaps of African Americans generally, depends upon deepening and enriching the culture that helped us survive and from whence we generate the strength to "keep on keeping on." It is futile to point out that the world is becoming smaller if it is moving every day in quite a different direction, away from black identity and consciousness. It has not yet arrived at the place where the particularities of race, color, and ethnicity have been effectively neutralized by technology and a global economy. As long as these ancient divisions are exacerbated by inequality and injustice people will either stumble over them in the unwise pursuit of vested interests or use them as battering rams to break down the walls that other vested interests have selfishly erected.

African American Christians want to join with others who are struggling to emerge from their own sub-floors and basements. It would be better if we would all join hands. But on the way to that necessary collaboration we cannot help but work in our own bumbling ways with what we have, in the spaces we happen to occupy, and with the comrades nearest at hand. If Fred Herzog were still around today I would say to him: "Have patience, my friend. It may take another hundred years!"

GUSTAVO GUTIÉRREZ

7. Liberation Theology and the Future of the Poor

As we face the end of the century, nostalgia and fears are inevitably evoked, accompanied by predictions as well as over-sights. To reflect on the role of the theological task in that context, however, is not an easily made concession to these sentiments and feelings. This type of reflection comes from a legitimate preoccupation with the Christian witness, a human situation that changes at a fast-moving pace, shaking the foundations of many of our preconceptions and of many historical projects. The subject invites two reflections that can lay important groundwork for the future.

Speaking of the next century, we have to speak about *time*, a reality full of expectation and meaning. From a biblical perspective, time is not something empty or abstract; instead we speak of what can be called inhabited time, inseparable from the people and events that comprise it. It is the theater where human activities occur. In that time, that is to say in the persons and the events that live and unfold within it, God communicates and reveals Godself as the foundation of love for all relationships with him and between human beings. In this manner, time acquires a density that is challenging and salvific. Far from being an abstract category or from being limited to a chronological registry of events, time converts itself into a place of encounter with the face of Jesus, God's incarnate Son. In this time two liberties meet: the liberty of God that reveals itself in gratuitous love, and the liberty of humanity which receives the gift; the first calls forth and establishes the second.

On the other hand, to question the task of the church and the understanding of faith for the next century means to ask ourselves, first of all, *what is this time telling us?* In order for the question to be truly fertile, it should be formulated from a specific moment and situation. We want to do this from within the Latin American experience. It has to do with God's saving presence today, upon which the biblical books of Deuteronomy and the Gospel of Luke so fervently insist. Pope John XXIII and the Second Vatican Council remind us of the importance of being attentive to the signs of the times. They constitute a summons to reflection and commitment. At this time we find ourselves before uncertain and particularly challenging signs. They therefore invite us to discern how to move to what is essential without becoming entangled in what is secondary or transitory, avoiding the trees that hide the forest. They call us to place ourselves before what is coming, beginning with the present.

Two convictions that will accompany the following pages are the dense theological time that confronts us and our need to be attentive to what it is telling us within an accelerated pace of history. After some consideration of the theological task and the criteria needed to look at the challenges presented by this new situation, we will try briefly to outline those questions, so that we may end the discussion by providing some guidance for the emerging era.

Theological Reflection

In the past few years we have been witnesses to a series of economic, political, cultural, and ecclesiastical events, both in the international arena and in Latin America. This might cause one to think that important aspects of the time that birthed and developed the reflection of what we call liberation theology since the late 1960s, have come to an end. Undoubtedly, the convulsive events within that period of Latin America were stimulating and creative, while at the same time, tense and conflicted. Faced with new situations, many of the statements and discussions of that period of time do not respond to today's challenges.

Liberation theology has much to learn from the new situation, from current events, from dialogue, and from theological as well as pastoral debate that took place during these years within the church. These events have purified the discussion about a closely held faith, born from a different reality and—why not?—from ideological permeations, brought about by the passage of time. There are, without a doubt, emphatic shifts, openings to other viewpoints, and modifications of attitudes that are important. What this situation demands is maturity and an ecclesiastical sense of reflection that does not lose sight of the realities and tasks it serves. Consequently, the road already traveled must be revisited in order to discern what is still essential and of value, often contained in the first intuitions, and what specific circumstances, not without confusion and diverse accents, have contributed to them.[1]

We will begin by putting some ideas in order with respect to this theological work.

Theology and Announcement

Faith is a gift. To receive this gift is to place yourself in the footsteps of Jesus, putting in practice his teaching and continuing his proclamation of God's realm. The point of departure of all theology is the act of faith. Thinking about faith is something that surges spontaneously from the believer, a reflection motivated by the desire to make the life of faith more profound and faithful. But it is not a purely individual matter; faith is always lived out within community. Both dimensions, the personal and the communal, mark the living out of faith, as well as its intellectual aspect.

The theological task is a vocation that is initiated and lived in the center of the ecclesiastical community. Theology serves the evangelizing mission of the church. Theology is to speak about God, driven by faith; God is, indeed, the first and last subject of theological language. Many other points can be made, but not without some measure of what they say in relation to God. God-talk presupposes, as Frederick Herzog taught us, a God-walk.[2]

The theological task is at the service of the truth, revealed by Jesus Christ, who is the truth. It is truth that liberates (cf. John 8:32) and that should be proclaimed. Christianity is not an esoteric religion. To be revealed, communicated (in the strong sense of creating community), belongs to the very essence of the Christian mystery (cf. Rom. 16: 25-26). In this task, theology needs to be aware that it cannot cover all the dimensions of the word present in the Scriptures, transmitted through tradition and taught by the magisterium. We are referring to the living memory of the church that Saint Irenaeus calls "the tradition of the truth" (*Adversus Haereses* III,4,1). All discourse about faith needs to be respectful of the mystery that surrounds it. In a way, theology should recognize that, like the prophet Jeremiah, "I do not know how to speak." (1:6).

It is for this reason that theological approximations are always insufficient. We must be willing to take new roads, to fine-tune notions, to modify the manner of approaching problems. Here we encounter the diversity, within the unity of the faith of the church, of the approximations to the revealed word throughout history. In effect, no theology identifies itself with faith, according to a traditional affirmation. The different attempts at an understanding of faith are useful and fertile, but only under the condition that none of them is taken as the only valid one. The meaning and the direction of these reflections demand a clear consciousness of the modest assistance they offer to the main duties of the church.

Theological reflection exists first and foremost to serve the Christian life and the evangelizing mission of the ecclesiastical community; but, for that very reason, it also constitutes a service to humanity. At the center of humanity, the church must proclaim its message in accessible and challenging language, taking into account the great human problems, as well as the actual presence of God's realm in its historical occurrence and its complete future realization. This perspective is one of the central themes of the Second Vatican Council. To evangelize is to announce with works and words the salvation in Christ. Having conquered the roots of the forces of sin that dominate the "former man" through his total commitment even unto death and his resurrection by the Father, the Son of God made flesh prepares the path for the "new man" in order to fulfill his vocation of communion with God "face to face" in the Pauline sense (1 Cor. 13).

But precisely because the freedom from sin goes to the very heart of human existence, where the freedom of each person is accepted or rejected, in the end nothing escapes the salvific action of Jesus Christ—the gratuitous and redeeming love of God. This love reaches all dimensions of humanity (personal and social) and puts its seal on it.

Liberation Theology

Obviously, everything that is said about the function of theology is valid for a specific theology. This is the case with liberation theology. Like all understanding of faith, liberation theology grows out of a precise location and moment, seeking to respond to historical situations that challenge, and at the same time, open new pathways for the evangelizing task of the church. The understanding of faith is permanent, therefore, when it relates to the effort at comprehension demanded by the gift of faith, but at the same time changeable when it responds to concrete questions and to a given cultural world.

Theologies bear the mark of the historical time and ecclesiastical context within which they are birthed. They live basically as long as the conditions that gave them their origins exist.[3] Naturally the great theologies somehow rise above these chronological and cultural boundaries, and those theologies of less breadth, no matter how significant they may have been in their time, are forever trapped in their circumstances and times. We refer, to be sure, to the particular modalities of a theology (immediate stimulus, instruments of analysis, philosophical and other notions), not to fundamental affirmations that concern revealed truths. The history of theology clearly illustrates what we have just pointed out.

On the other hand, it should be observed that all theological reflection, even with its limits and deficiencies, its passions and inconclusive intents, enters into dialogue with other aspects of the understanding of faith present in the Christian community. The characteristic of a theology is to help clarify the consciousness of the believer in relation to the believer's encounter with God and what the Good News implies for the world. Each theology does it with its resources and its limits; it is enriched with the help of other theologies and contributes to them. The most important thing for a discussion of faith is not duration, and even less perpetuation; but rather, like a stream, it should carry its waters to fuller and broader rivers in the life of the church, which runs through human history.

What should interest us more than the present and future of a specific theology are the suffering and anguish, the joy and hope of people today, and the current situation of the evangelizing task of the church. This is one of the pillars that sustains liberation theology which has always underscored itself as a secondary act in relation to the first act constituted by the encounter with God and others in prayer and commitment to history.

An Evangelical Standard. It is well known that, from its beginnings, liberation theology, born from an intense pastoral preoccupation, has been attached to the life of the church, to the celebration of the community, its evangelizing restlessness, and its solidarity with the Latin American society—in particular with the poorest of its members. The Latin American Bishops' Conferences of these decades (Medellín, Puebla, Santo Domingo), many texts of national dioceses, and other documents uphold this assertion, even when they invite us to provide critical discernment of unfounded affirmations and positions that some pretended to deduce from this theological perspective.

The fundamental contribution of liberation theology, it seems, revolves around the so-called preferential option for the poor. This concern is about an option that is radically evangelical, and because of this, it constitutes an important criterion through which to discern the rapid events and modes of thinking of our current times.

The proposal put forth by Pope John XXIII regarding "the church for all and especially the church of the poor"[4] found fertile ground in Latin America. Our continent is the only one that is predominantly Christian and poor at the same time. The presence of massive and inhuman poverty raised the question of the biblical significance of poverty. Toward the middle of the decade of the sixties, between Vatican II and Medellín (1968), three distinct definitions of the term poor were formulated: (1) *real* poverty (frequently called material poverty) as a scandalous state not desired by God; (2) *spiritual* poverty, spiritual childhood, an expression of which—not the only one—is the lack of interest in the material goods of this world; (3) poverty as a *commitment*: solidarity with the poor and protest against poverty.

Medellín took up this distinction with authority; it became enormously significant in the life of the Latin American church and beyond. This focus inspired commitment and reflection by many Christian communities and became the foundation of that which, around the time of Puebla and the writings of this episcopal conference, would be captured in the phrase "preferential option for the poor." In effect, what we find in the three terms of this phrase, one by one, are the three notions distinguished by Medellín. Later the conference held in Santo Domingo would reaffirm this option, in which we should be inspired "for every action that is evangelistic, communal and personal" (n. 178).

This formulation—which led to a reappropriation of one piercing biblical phrase—created its pathway and today is universally found in the ecclesiastical magisterium and in numerous and diverse texts within Christian communities. It is present in a particular way, providing inspiration and courage to many commitments.[5]

Grace, the foundation of preference. The theme of poverty and marginalization invites us to speak about justice and to have before us our Christian duties. Yet we do not have to lose sight of what makes the preferential option for the poor a central theme: at its root is the gratuitous love of God. This is the ultimate foundation of preference.

The word *preference* itself rejects all exclusivity and searches to underline those who should be the first—not the only ones— in our solidarity. Commenting on the meaning of preference is a frequent discussion topic, and the great challenge comes from the necessity of simultaneously maintaining the universal nature of God's love and God's preference for the lesser ones of history. To remain only with one of these extremes is to mutilate the gospel message.

Ultimately it is important to emphasize that the option for the poor is an option for God's realm, which Jesus announces. The definitive reason for commitment with the poor and the oppressed is not, consequently, in the social analysis that we employ, nor in the direct experience that we may have with poverty, nor in our own human compassion. All of those are valid motives that without a doubt play a significant role in our lives and reasons for our solidarity. Yet for Christians this solidarity is based fundamentally in faith in the God of Jesus Christ. It is a *theocentric* and prophetic *option* that sinks its roots into the gratuitous love of God and is required by it. There is nothing more demanding, we know, than gratitude (cf. Paul's Letter to Philemon).

The poor need to be preferred, not because they are necessarily better than others from a moral or religious point of view, but because God is God. The entire Bible is marked by the love of God favoring the weak and the mistreated in human history. This is revealed to us in the Beatitudes of the Gospel. With frightening simplicity, the Beatitudes tell us that the preference for the poor, the hungry, and the suffering has its foundation in God's gratuitous love.[6] Because of this, the preferential option for the poor is not simply a pastoral rule or guide, or a perspective for reflecting theologically, but it is also, indeed most of all, *a spiritual way of life* in the strongest sense of the phrase. It is an itinerary of an encounter with God and the gratuity of God's love, a "walk before the Lord in the land of the living" (Ps. 116:9). If we do not reach this level of spirituality in following Jesus, that is, seeing it as being at the heart of the Christian life, the significance and fecundity of this decision will not be perceived.

A philosopher of deep biblical (and talmudic) roots has developed a thought, more concretely, an ethic (for him the primary kind of philosophy), of the change that can illuminate our consideration. I allude to Emmanuel Levinas.[7] "The Bible," he tells us, "is about the priority of the other in relation to the self." What is valid for each person is made even more radical when you speak of the poor. "In the other," he continues, "I always see the widow and the orphan. The other always goes before the self."[8] The widow, the orphan, and the stranger constitute the trilogy that the Bible designates as the poor.

This perception, deeply rooted in the Bible, clearly maintains the distinction between God and human beings, but it does not separate them. The commitment with the poor is not limited only to the social sphere; that is obviously present, but it also includes, as something primordial, a profound spiritual content and christological foundation. It has a close and indissoluble relation to the basic truths of our faith. Only on this backdrop is the significance of the preferential option for the poor appreciated. This is how many Christians in Latin America have lived and are living. That is why it becomes a principal and fruitful criterion for understanding these current times from the standpoint of faith.[9] The fortune and the significance of liberation theology are closely linked to the significance of the preferential option for the poor in the Christian life.

The Poor and the Future

We have alluded on various occasions to an event that today gathers a large consensus: diverse factors have led in the last years to a radical mutation of the living conditions of humanity. This may be more evident in certain regions of the world; but, in one way or another, no region escapes the vertigo of what some consider a new period in history (there is no lack of those who with involuntary humor proclaim "the end of history...").

We do not yet have the necessary historical distance to evaluate in a definitive way the times in which we live. There is no doubt, however, about the unique aspect of the state of affairs: a situation that makes us rethink many subjects. Various analyses and proposals announced in recent years have lost their validity; numerous discussions and precisions of that time do not fully respond to the current challenges. To ignore these changes would mean to be enclosed in the past, to live nostalgically and to be condemned to live with our backs turned to the people of today's world. This is not about a frivolous attempt to be "up-to-date" but a matter of being serious regarding the solidarity and attention that we owe to others. Furthermore, for a Christian it means to remain open to what God wants to tell us through these historical events from within the perspective of the signs of the times that we mentioned in previous pages.

A brief text of the book of Exodus can illuminate this purpose. Among the rules of the covenant that Moses receives from Yahweh to be transmitted to the people is one that asks where the people who do not have shelter will sleep (cf. Ex. 22:26). The text, situated in the perspective of the year of Jubilee, invites us to formulate a question that can help us see what is currently at stake: *Where will the poor sleep* in the world that is emerging, and to a certain degree, has already emerged? What will become of those favored by God in the world that is to come?

Toward a Fascinating and Cruel Century

Recently, Enrique Iglesias, president of the International Development Bank (IDB), said that the upcoming century would be "a fascinating and cruel century." Like all phrases that are somewhat paradoxical, this one is especially challenging and attractive. Nevertheless, if we take the time to read it closer, it reveals the tragic reality it expresses.

Thanks to the extraordinary development of science and technology, a fascinating era is opening up. An era that provides the possibilities of communication (or at least of information) between persons, the likes of which humanity has never seen, also provides capability of dominion over nature that supersedes the limits of our planet and creates realities that until recently seemed to be science fiction. With these possibilities comes the opportunity for unlimited consumption and, unfortunately, a potential for destruction that can reach all of humanity. As human beings and believers we value and admire these advances, yet we cannot keep from being aware of the dark clouds that are also forming on the horizon.

To sum up, the time ahead will be fascinating for persons who posses a certain social status and who participate in the latest advancement of technological knowledge. Those who have that opportunity tend to form an international human establishment, closed within itself and forgetful of those who do not form part of their club; forgetful of even the members of their own countries. The latter are the poor. The second adjective of the phrase applies basically to the poor. The next century will be cruel for those who are "insignificant" in history. Their poverty and marginalization—if we do not make an enormous effort of solidarity with them—will increase; there will be greater misery and their number will grow, as all the statistics compiled by international organizations forecast.

In other words, the immediate future will not, in fact, be fascinating and cruel for the same persons. This makes the challenge facing our present times even more pressing and makes stronger the demand of faith that the God of Jesus Christ, who loves all and who calls us to protect the least of these, imposes on us.

A market without restrictions. We live in a time that is more and more dominated by the liberal economy, or neoliberal, if you prefer. It is a market without restrictions, called to regulate itself by its own means. This is the principle, almost absolute, of the economic life. The celebrated and classic "laissez-faire" of the beginnings of liberal economy today postulate in a universal form—at least in theory—that all intervention by political power, even if to attend to social needs, is detrimental to economic growth and is harmful to all. For this reason, if there are any difficulties that face economic progress, the only solution is to have more markets.

After some changes, the liberal wave has recently regained strength and seems to grow without restrictions. The great multinational corporations (the dominant element of the present economic order) and the rich nations pressure the poorer nations to open their markets, privatize their economies and make what have been called structural adjustments. International organizations (the World Bank, the International Monetary Fund) have been efficient agents in the integration of weakened economies into a single market. Although the awareness of interdependency contains much that is positive, its current revisions form an asymmetry that exacerbates existing unjust inequalities. The latest element of the "globalization" of the economy is the financial capital that navigates through the world, crossing frontiers with an incredible mobility in search of new and better profits. The national economies—even those of the large countries—are being erased.[10]

Diverse factors have intervened in the process that has brought this result. Without a doubt, at the political level, one factor has been the fall of authoritarian socialism in Russia and the countries of the Eastern bloc, which failed to see the complexities of the human dimension and systematically violated the right of freedom. From a bipolar world we have moved to a unipolar world, more in regard to political and military matters, of course, than to economical ones. Another factor of great impact is the role that technological knowledge has attained (new materials, new sources of energy, and biotechnology); one of the more dynamic of these is the computer industry.[11] The matter has brought noticeable changes in production. It is becoming clearer every day that knowledge has become the most important axis for wealth accumulation in the economic sphere. Advances in this area have permitted an acceleration of the already unfettered exploitation and depravation of natural resources of our planet, humanity's common possession.

With its achievements and violent acts, its progress and cruelty, its possibilities and what it has forgotten, the economic panorama and the contemporary social fabric have changed in recent years at a dizzying pace, the likes of which have not been seen in centuries. The new situation calls for a renewal of methods of analysis that allow us to account for the multiple factors at play in the social and economic framework of our time.[12] It also calls us to consider these changes from a Christian ethical perspective and from a theological reflection in search of discernment.

Ethics and the economy. Does ethics, and more specifically, does a Christian ethic, have something to say to the world about the economy?

The question would not have had any meaning in the sixteenth century. Caught by surprise, the moral theologians of that era (Francisco de Vitoria among them) who occupied themselves with matters of the then-emerging capitalism, which sometimes has been called mercantile capitalism, only dared to say that the answer was obviously affirmative. But the modern economy challenges the moral norms that are communally accepted and not only in circles that we call traditional. Jealousy, selfishness, and greed become engines for the economy. Solidarity, concern for the poor, is seen as a barrier to economic growth, counterproductive to achieving a general well-being from which all could benefit some day.

Some shrewd economists of the liberal tradition were aware of this collision of values, but they accepted it, because they saw in it something necessary and inevitable. A case in point is J.M. Keynes, who in a text from 1928–1930, affirmed with horrifying clarity: "When accumulation no longer has such social importance . . . we will be able to free ourselves from many of the pseudomoral principles that we have had to take upon ourselves for two hundred years. . . . The love of money as a possession . . . will be known for what it really is: something morbid and unpleasant."[13]

The moment will come, thought Keynes, when it will be possible to name things for what they are and to say "that avarice is a vice and the practice of usury is a crime and the love of money is something detestable." But with disenchanted and uneasy resignation he holds: "Beware! We are not there yet. For at least one hundred years we have to pretend to ourselves and to everyone else that what is just is evil and what is evil is just." The reason for this inversion of values is that "the unjust is useful and the just is not. Avarice, usury and wariness must be our gods for a little while longer. In effect, only they can lead us out of the tunnel of economic need toward the light of day."[14]

This is not a new theme and it has been dealt with on many occasions; the great number of current studies on the subject is proof of the importance of studying the basis of economics from an ethical and theological perspective and, to be precise, from the preferential option for the poor. One should certainly respect the autonomy of a discipline that attempts to know as strictly as possible the field of economic activity. In the past, many incorrect roads have been taken, and it is necessary to learn from this experience. But this does not mean that the economy is a sector absolutely independent from the rest of existence, just as it is not the core or the totality of it. Economic movement must necessarily be placed and examined within the context of human life in its entirety and by the light of faith. Immediate effectiveness is not definitive.

Today studies about necessary ethical rules or guidelines for economic activities are multiplying. They come from different perspectives, especially with regard to the religious perversion expressed in certain justifications of the economy as centered in forces that do not restrict the market. Values of freedom, personal initiatives, the possibilities for technological progress, as well as the function that these can play in the market within certain parameters, are all recognized. But the logic of the market is denounced; it subdues people, countries and cultures through its effort at homogenizing, as well as through the new fractures within the social fabric that it provokes. Also questioned is the hypocrisy of an economic liberalism that does not feel appalled by dictatorships or totalitarian governments and that with great ease separates economic freedom from other freedoms.[15]

In this context it is most interesting that the exclusion of the poorest is irrelevant to the dominant economic system. The following section is dedicated to this matter.

Insignificance and Exclusion

The Gospel according to Luke brings us a challenging parable of which we only want to recall two phrases: "There was a rich man . . ." and "at his gate lay a poor man . . ." (16:19-20). This is the situation of humanity today. The poor nations are lying next to the rich nations, ignored by these; but we must add that the gap between the two is greater every day. The same occurs within each country. Increasingly the world population is being placed at either end of the economic and social spectrum.

The challenge of poverty. Liberation theology was born from the challenge that faith must represent the massive and inhuman poverty that exists in Latin America and the Caribbean.[16] For this reason its first studies were a reflection on the biblical significance of the different types of poverty and a consideration, in the light of faith, of the evangelizing obligation of Christians, and of all of the church for the poor. Numerous questions can be raised about later developments of this theological line of thought and about the social analyses that were used to understand the reality of poverty and its causes. But, for the moment, in deference to our topic, let us simply ask ourselves, in what way is the challenge of poverty presented to the Christian conscience in today's world?

A first look shows that this matter has become worse. The 1996 report of the United Nations on development contains troubling statistics. The conclusion is that "the world is more polarized each day, and the distance that separates the poor from the rich is growing greater each day."[17] Something similar is happening within each country, including the rich nations. This and other data cause one to see that, in relative and absolute terms, the population finds itself in a situation of poverty, extreme poverty.[18] The result is shameful: in most developing countries poverty is maintained and even increased. Consequently, the challenge to our solidarity and our reflection remains strongly valid today.

One expression of the worsening of events just mentioned is the so-called economic and social exclusion. It is not a reality or an analytical category that is totally new. In one way or another the poor have always been excluded and marginalized (think about the indigenous and black population in Latin America and the Caribbean, for example). But this should not keep us from perceiving what is distinctive at the present moment. The notion of social exclusion has various dimensions. At the economic level the new methods of production, due in great part to the revolution in knowledge, cause a devaluation of raw materials with detrimental consequences for poor countries. Under this situation the labor market depends entirely on the technical qualification of the worker, thereby excluding the great majority of the poor today. Exclusion in the world of politics (lack of participation in the decisions that are made in this environment) and in culture (racial and gender discrimination) reinforce the economic exclusion.

These events have allowed two sectors of humanity to emerge. One of these, the sector of the excluded ones, is less relevant each day to the functioning of the world economy and society which solidifies itself more and more. That is why, for many years, in liberation theology we have spoken of the poor as "insignificant ones," meaning that their social location excludes them from the dominant circles. This term allows us to remember, further, that for the believer in the God who does not make any exception of persons, no one can be deemed insignificant.

From the viewpoint of the poor. Inspired by the universal magisterium of the church, the North American bishops put forth a few years ago a criterion by which to judge a particular political economy. Alluding to the option for the poor and the need to evaluate social and economic activity "from the point of view of the poor," they affirmed: "If society is going to achieve justice for *all*, it must recognize the priority of vindicating those who are marginalized and those whose rights are denied."[19] The repercussions for the weaker ones are a criterion to decide whether justice exists in a society.[20]

This is an important point of view, especially if one takes into consideration that those who are marginalized are often victims of a socioeconomic system. The Latin American experience has enabled us to understand that, in the end, poverty means death: early and unjust death. Poverty is a reality of the economic and social order. But if we remain on these levels we do not perceive the radical event that is at stake in poverty: the life and death of persons. Poverty, as we know it in our world today, is a global matter that summons the entire human conscience and a Christian concept of life.

During his visit to Canada, Pope John Paul II alluded to the text in Matt. 25:31-46, which is pertinent for our theme: "In the light of the words of Christ, this poor South shall judge the opulent North. The poor people and the poor nations—poor in different ways, not only lacking food, but also lacking freedom and other human rights—shall judge those who take away these goods by force, in order to accumulate for themselves an imperialistic monopoly of economic and political predominance at the expense of the other."[21]

Before concluding, it is important to remember that the poor, the insignificant, and excluded are not passive persons waiting for someone to extend them a hand. Not only do they have needs, but within them boil many human riches and possibilities. The poor and marginalized in Latin America often possess a culture with eloquent values coming from their people, their own history, and their own language. They have energy, as demonstrated by women's organizations from all around the continent as they struggle for the life of their families and of the poor with an inventive and creative force, which is impressive in its ability to confront crisis. The Christian faith has played an important role among the poor of Latin America; it has been a fountain of inspiration and a powerful reason not to deny themselves hope for the future.

The Weakening of Thought

The historical era we are entering is complex. Cultural aspects are added to the economic and political ones and equally shape contemporary mentality. This is a reference to what some people call postmodernity or postmodern thought. We are conscious of the ambiguity of the concept of postmodernity, and above all of the name, but it undoubtedly corresponds to an aspect of reality.

It is better to mention at the beginning that we are referring to an issue confined to intellectual minorities, although it is in these circles that this perspective is mostly present. Neither should it be thought that it is limited to Europe and North America, although—once again—this is where this subject is discussed and written about more often. The media, art, literature, and also certain theologies, transmit some of their concepts beyond the intellectual environments of countries still known as the Third World, while at the same time shaping many attitudes. Some of those concepts strengthen aspects of the neglect of the insignificant ones of this world that we addressed above in terms of neoliberalism. Others, of course, can open new perspectives on the topic that we are discussing.

It is not pointless, therefore, to deal with the question that may serve as the guiding thread for the following pages: Where will the poor of this postmodern world (or however you would like to call it) sleep? The attempt to respond to this query will help outline clearly the steps to take from the point of view of Christian witness.

Controversial modernity. We will not enter the debate of whether we are really in an historical era that can be called postmodernity or if it is a new phase of modernity. The matter has been much discussed and a great variety of opinions exist. But as we have said earlier, it is certain that there are aspects of reality that are emphasized by these perspectives and these merit a certain consideration. There are ambivalent feelings and issues difficult to clarify; there are, however, also profiles that trace a particular moment of thought and of human conduct in daily living that for convenience—and without too much conviction—we shall call postmodern.

We are facing a reaction against some of the great themes of modernity, specifically against what the representatives of this thought call the "grand narratives" (or metanarratives) of modernity.[22] J. F. Lyotard lists them as follows: "Progressive emancipation of reason and of freedom, progressive emancipation or the catastrophe of work (source of alienated value in capitalism), enrichment of all of humanity through the progress of capitalistic techno-science." The author adds, and this is important for us: "This includes, if you take into account Christianity within modernity (in opposition, therefore, to the old classicism), salvation of creatures through the conversion of souls by way of the mystical narrative of martyred love."[23]

What is rejected head-on is "the philosophy of Hegel [that] totalizes all of these narratives and, in a sense, is the center of speculative modernity."[24] For this author the justification of knowledge through metanarrative implies a philosophy of history.[25] What is rejected is the will to power that the grand narratives of modernity represent. What is more, the postmoderns see in this attitude an act of violence that takes away freedom from individuals, and for that reason must be rejected.

All unified conceptions of history remain, therefore, off track.[26] It does not make sense to organize events of the human world under the idea of a universal human history, a history whose development is in a certain way known beforehand. We only have small narratives, individual and local histories. There are no metaphysical foundations of the evolution of history. We are facing what has been called a fragmentation of human knowledge.

A consequence of these premises is that many opinions have room within postmodernity. Within it is an enormous pluralism that has led to the belief that in this way of thinking "anything goes."[27] Reacting against positions that consider themselves dog-matic and totalitarian, we arrive at a cultural relativism, colored by a certain skepticism in regard to the possibilities of knowing the human being. This skepticism has repercussions, not only in ethics but also in politics.

Without a doubt, the postmodern critique emphasizes the weaknesses and also the contradictions of modernity. It needs to be remembered, however, that modern thought always cultivates self-criticism: more than one of its proponents expressed dissat-isfaction with the results of the Enlightenment. But now the cri-tique is much more radical, and what is more, it has crossed the bounds of intellectual circles, inasmuch as an attitude about life reaches diverse social sectors, some of which play a very active role in the cultural environment and in the communication of contemporary society.

The fragmentation of human knowledge. There is, without doubt, something healthy in the reaction against totalizing visions of history that form grand narratives. These perspectives involve an authoritarianism that has been well seen by post-modernists. The poor have often seen themselves manipulated by projects that pretend to be global without consideration for people and their daily lives, and because they are intensely ori-ented toward the future they forget the present. But modern thought does not limit itself to this; it also erodes all sense of his-tory and has repercussions for the significance to be given to every human existence. Furthermore, it identifies G. W. F. Hegel's philosophy of history with the Judeo-Christian concept of history, and rejects both.

It is fair to recognize that the postmodern critique helps us to keep from falling into rigidly starched schematics while inter-preting the course of history. This has often happened inside the theological world. Nevertheless, having said this, it is necessary to remember that a Christian perspective on history has its center in the coming of the Son, in the Incarnation, without meaning that human history advances inevitably on pathways blazed and dom-inated by a single rule of thinking. Jesus Christ as the center of history is also the Way (cf. John 14:6) toward the Father. This walk gives meaning to the human existence to which we are called. This vocation gives full density to the present, to the here and now, as we have argued in the introductory pages of this chapter.

But we cannot avoid the fact that this sensibility is connected to an exacerbation of individualism present in modernity. The negation of the sense of history gives rise to individualism and reinforces the narcissistic nature of today's society.[28] In this regard some have spoken of a second individualistic revolution. It would be necessary to make sure that the critique of the project of modernity does not cover up a willingness to find refuge in individualism and in an indifference to others that would promote a society enclosed in itself. The postmodern critique pretends an overcoming of modernity, critiquing many aspects of which liberation theology has always been very critical, but in a different optic from this theology.

Contrary to what the modern mentality thought, religion has not only not become exhausted or reduced to the private space, but rather it presents a new vitality. The postmodern disposition can contribute to respect for the mystery and give support to what some consider an emergence of a new religious era. The examples are multiple in today's world. We should observe, however, that what is emerging is a diffuse and confused religiosity, a carrier of a generic belief about God, mistrusting firm convictions and resilient to the demands of behavior that these convictions require. It will be necessary to bear in mind this current reality from the perspective of faith.

If to this is added skepticism, which believes that all opinions are of equal value and that each one has—as it is frequently said today—*its* truth, anything goes. The reaction against global visions—in spite of what they have that is healthy—makes us eliminate from view all utopias or alternative projects to what exists at the present time. It goes without saying that the first victims of these attitudes are the poor and marginalized, for whom very little space appears to be created in the world. It is always easy to criticize utopias from unchanging *ivory towers* where one is completely satisfied.

However, as we have already indicated, to be vigilant in regard to the significance of our present time and to know how to discern it, one must not forget values that are found in this mentality as well. In this complex and sometimes even contradictory situation, it is necessary to give witness to God's realm, to solidarity with the poor, and to the liberation of those whose most basic rights are violated. To reflect on these events in the light of faith is to do theology.

Liberated to Be Free

It is opportune to make some brief observations about the relationship between liberation and freedom, central themes in the theology of liberation.[29] The point of departure is based on Paul's important text in the Letter to the Galatians, which is centered on the theme of Christian freedom. "For freedom Christ has set us free," says Paul (5:1). Liberation is from sin, which greedily folds over itself. To sin is to deny loving God and others. For Paul this implies also freedom from the Law and the forces of death (cf. Rom. 8:2). Sin, which ruptures the friendship with God and others, is, in the Bible, the ultimate cause of injustice and oppression between human beings, and it is also the lack of real personal freedom.[30] It is ultimate, because there are other causes at the level of economic and social structures, as well as in the personal dimensions. Any transformation of these conditions, as radical as it may be, is not enough. Only the freely given and salvific love of Christ can go to the root of ourselves and from there cause a true love to break forth.

Nevertheless, Paul does not limit himself to saying that Christ liberated us; he equally affirms what Christ did so that we could be free. According to a classical distinction, it is necessary to consider a freedom *from* and a freedom *for*. The former points to sin, to greed, to oppression, to injustice, to need; conditions that all require liberation. The latter points to the reason for this freedom: love, that is, communion, is the final stage of liberation. *Freedom for* gives a profound meaning to *freedom from*. If we appeal to what is said in the same letter (5:13), we could say that the expression *free to love* synthesizes the Pauline position. Without a reflection on freedom, a theology of liberation remains crippled.

Freedom is a central element of the Christian message. The accent on liberation must not cause this to be forgotten. It is important to establish a fertile relationship between liberation and freedom. The matter becomes even more urgent before certain challenges of our current times. These problems lead us to underscore the importance of another valuable aspect of faith that is strictly tied to the theme of freedom. We refer to the relationship that Scripture establishes between truth and liberty. "The truth shall set you free," says the well known text in the Gospel of John (8:32). That truth is Christ himself, who liberates us and calls us to freedom (cf. Gal. 5:13). The evangelizing task of the church must make persons really free, free to love.

Seek the Kingdom and Justice

At the heart of the Sermon on the Mount is a verse that in a certain way sums up the entire sermon: "Seek first God's kingdom and God's justice, and all these things will be given to you as well" (Matt. 6:33). The subject of the two possessives of the first phrase is in the previous verse: it is the "heavenly father."

The reason for this search lies in the Christian life. In a precise manner and with challenges that are important to take into account, Matthew presents us the marrow of the entire Bible: God alone. God is the holy One, the complete Other, the One of whom it is said that "unsearchable are his judgment and inscrutable are his ways . . . because from him and for him are all things" (Rom. 11:33, 35). God is the fountain of life and love (cf. Exod. 3:14; 1 John 4:16), a distant and at the same time close God who calls us into friendship. This friendship with God is the foundation of the friendship that should exist between all human beings. This holy God is also the God incarnate. To receive God's love in our lives must translate itself into gestures of life to others.

In the face-to-face encounter with God (1 Cor. 13:12) human existence reaches it fulness. This is the hope and experience of the mystics, the union with God that is often spoken of. "My eye sees you," proclaims Job (42:5) when he understands that the gratuitous love of God, without limits or shortcuts, is the foundation of the world, and not his narrow concept of a justice of "you scratch my back, I'll scratch yours." Arriving at the end of the journey, St. John of the Cross poetically states, "I remained, lost in oblivion; my face I reclined on my beloved . . . forgotten among the lilies."[31] The mystical experience has always found in poetry the most appropriate language to express the mystery of love.

Nothing is more contrary to the search for God, God's realm, and justice than service (in the strong sense of the word: worship) of an idol fabricated by human hands. Idolatry according to the Bible is to give one's life and put one's trust in someone or something that is not God. It is a permanent risk for Christians. As we have seen, in the neoliberal context, the market and the profit are objects of idolatrous worship. For this reason, John Paul II talks about "the idolatry of the market" (*CA* 40). It is the contemporary form of the worship of Mammon. Added to the idolatry of money is that of power that overrides all human rights. To those idols an offering of victims is made, so that the biblical prophets always link idolatry with murder. Those excluded in the present international economic order are among these victims.

It is necessary to go further yet.[32] The idolatrous aspects of the worship of money and the will to power, unfortunately, are clear and massive in our days and are repugnant to human and Christian conscience. The idolatrous attitude, however, can also enter through the back door of our commitment to the liberation of the poor, in spite of how well-intended it may be and how well-inspired by the Christian faith it is presented. To affirm this may seem strange at first glance, but it is necessary to see things without exaggerations or evasions.

It is possible, for example, to turn justice into something like an idol if we make it absolute and do not know how to place it within the context that permits it to release all of its meaning: the meaning of gratuitous love. If there is no daily friendship with the poor nor any value placed on the diversity of their desires and needs, then, being human, we can—it seems cruel to say this but experience teaches us—transform the search for justice into a pretext, and even into a justification, to mistreat the poor, pretending to know better than they what they need and what they desire.

We can also make of the poor a kind of idol. This happens when we idealize them, considering them *always good*, generous, profoundly religious, thinking that everything that comes from the poor is true and in a certain manner sacred. This quality of the poor can be converted into the principal reason for solidarity with them. In this way we can overlook that the poor are human beings, and as such they participate in grace and sin, as St. Augustine would say. That among the poor there can be enormous doses of generosity and commitment is something that cannot be disputed. But to go from there to say that this is true in all cases is to forget about human complexity and ambiguity. The idealization of the poor—by those who are not poor, and sometimes by the very same poor—is not conducive to their liberation. Furthermore, and above all, it is necessary to remember that for a Christian the ultimate reason for solidarity with the poor is not based on their moral and religious qualifications—although these exist—but rather in the goodness of God that must inspire our own conduct.

In a more subtle form, our own theology can also become an idol, including the theology of liberation that we try to do in Latin America, beginning with the suffering and hopes of the poor. This happens when theology becomes more important than the faith which illuminates it and the reality it tries to express. This is the risk that every intellectual task carries within itself. We do well to remember that the first witnesses of the Latin American Church who wanted to manifest their faith in the God of the Bible through solidarity with the poor are those who live oftentimes anonymously, risking their lives in pastoral and social commitment in daily struggles. They are anonymous for the media, but not for God.

That is why the topic of spirituality has been, from the beginning, central to the theology of liberation, at least to a large part of it. Here we deal with reflection of faith that is placed in the tension between mysticism and historical commitment.[33] As we have recalled above, the preferential option for the poor to which such theology is related, is a theocentric option.

Identity and Dialogue

The question of the other is an old subject in the frame of liberation theology, which has seen the poor as the insignificant "other" of a society that becomes more and more satisfied with itself. It is indisputable that we live in a time when distances on our planet earth are becoming shorter; at the same time, there is growing awareness of the diversity of cities, cultures, genders, ethnicities, and religion. These are not contradictory movements, as one might think. In a certain sense they support each other; although at times they do meet head on and produce dangerous whirlpools.

In Latin America the old indigenous cultures have made their voice of protest known through the taunts delivered for many centuries. But they have also raised their voice to enrich others with the abundance of their culture; their love for the land as fountain of life; their respect, through experience, for the natural world; their sense of community; and the depth of their religious values. With their own unique experiences, something similar occurs with the black population of our continent, with the new presence of women, especially those who belong to the marginalized and oppressed sectors of society. From them comes a rich and promising theological reflection.[34]

It is important to distinguish between these groups, for they are not uniform cells. It is also necessary to take into consideration the growing affirmation of the people's values that results from the recent mixing that is taking place in this continent of "all bloods," as José María Arguedas said, referring to Peru. We not only have in mind the racial situation but also the cultural aspect, and culture is permanently evolving. In effect, culture does not belong to the past; it is a continuous creation, faithful yet open in respect to a tradition. From here comes its capacity to resist postures and ideas that try to dissolve its identity. The past and present of the people—of all the peoples—of our continent are full of examples.

On another matter, as we have already pointed out, the postmodern disposition, which is full of ambiguities toward different social levels, tends to appreciate what is local and different. We cannot overlook, however, that this is often done from a skeptical point of view that relativizes any possibility of attaining universal truths.

To announce the Good News is to establish a salvific dialogue. It supposes the respect for the other and his or her peculiarities. It does not want to impose itself but to serve and to persuade. This points to what we call today the inculturation of faith and, without a doubt, it corresponds to an old experience of the church. It is a double movement: the Christian faith should constantly be incarnated within new cultural values; at the same time, it can be said that cultures must assume the evangelical message.

It is, however, important to note that dialogue implies interlocutors conscious of their own identity. Christian faith and theology cannot renounce their sources and character in order to establish contact with other points of view. To have firm convictions is not an obstacle to dialogue. It is, rather, a necessary condition. To receive, not by one's own merit, but through the grace of God the truth of Jesus Christ in our lives does not invalidate our relationship with persons and other perspectives, but rather gives these relationships authenticity.

What we have just said seems to be obvious, but we have to keep in mind that tendency which we see today in many persons and Christians who believe that authentic dialogue cannot occur if in some way each party does not renounce their beliefs and understanding of truth. This attitude comes from fear—which unfortunately can be illustrated with numerous historical cases—of imposing a Christian point of view by force. But it is also clear that skepticism, relativism, "the weak thought," do not find adequate language for a dialogue that is truly respectful and fruitful. The great challenge is to know how to enter into dialogue without hiding or denying the truths that we believe in. It is a demand of faith and honesty.[35] But once more, having said that, it is necessary to have a great capacity to listen and an openness to what God can tell us from other human and cultural perspectives. Paradoxically, the capability to listen to others is only as great as our own convictions are strong and as our Christian identity is transparent.

Today the preferential option for the poor and those excluded is a central element of Christian and ecclesial identity. Its reference to the heavenly father who bestows the gift of his kingdom and justice is basic; its christological foundation is clear and evident, it carries the seal of love and freedom that the Holy Spirit brings to us. In this manner it contributes, rooted properly in the Christian message, to the initiation of a dialogue with other perspectives at the center of the ecclesiastical community and outside it.

An ethic of solidarity

The indigenous people of Latin America have a secular practice of solidarity and reciprocity. We have in mind, for example, the way in which the members of a community share labor. There is much to learn from this experience that does not belong only to the past but holds a living model for today.

Furthermore, in recent times, the term "solidarity" and reflection upon it are frequent themes in this continent. For Christians, solidarity expresses an effective love for all and, in particular, for the weak ones in society. At stake are not only personal gestures, because solidarity is also a social demand that signifies an obligation for the whole church.

Two aspects of the perspective of solidarity are particularly relevant to our commitment and our theological reflection. The first concerns the actualization and depth of a theme of various bibli-cal and patristic roots: the universal use of the goods of the earth. Today, more than ever, is the time to remember that God has given to all humanity what is necessary for its sustenance. The goods of this earth do not belong exclusively to certain persons or to certain social groups, whatever their knowledge or place in society may be. The goods belong to all. Only within this frame-work is it acceptable to appropriate privately what is needed for survival and to create a better social order. We can call this a utopian perspective, but in a realistic sense of the word, which rejects an inhuman situation and pursues relationships of justice and cooperation between persons.

The second consequence of solidarity that we want to point out regards the difficult problem of the foreign debt. It is clear that the poor countries can pay their debt only at a very high cost: the very life and pain of enormous sectors of their population. This is an ethical issue. In some fashion all economic problems that are important and that affect the life of persons are ethical mat-ters, but in regard to the debt, we are faced with something so evident that it is monstrous to pretend that this problem is mere-ly technical. Without doubt the responsibilities are shared. It is true that the crisis of the 1970s pushed international agencies, banks, and nations to invest their money in poor nations; we cannot deny the responsibility of the political leaders and those who controlled the economy of the developing nations. But it is also evident that repayment of this debt will leave—is already leaving—millions of poor people without a place to sleep. Many arguments can be made for the forgiveness of the debt, but the most decisive is the ethical one: the life and death of so many per-sons.

A theology of life

Poverty, as we have referred to it above, ultimately means death: the physical death of many persons and the cultural death through neglect of so many others.[36] Two decades ago, the per-ception of this situation caused the theme of life, which is a gift of the God of our faith, to strongly emerge among us. The early events of Christians being murdered because of their testimony transformed this into a much more urgent concern. Reflection on the experience of persecution and martyrdom has given strength and depth to a theology of life, allowing us to understand that the option for the poorest is an option for life.

On the other hand, the experience of these years has also broadened the perspective on social solidarity. This experience should include the importance of a respectful relationship with nature. The ecological issue does not affect only industrial countries, those who are responsible for the major destruction of the natural habitat of the human species. It touches all of humanity, as many studies and numerous ecclesial texts have made clear. It is said with good reason that the planet Earth is like a large ship in which we are all passengers. Nevertheless, this same image can serve to remind us that in this common ship there are those who travel first class and those who travel third class. No one escapes the task of preventing the destruction of life in our natural habitat, but from our countries we should be attentive to how it affects the weakest members of humanity. And we should reaffirm our faith in the God of life, above all among those people who have always held the earth sacred.

This perspective can reclaim the corrections which the Bible introduces to abusive interpretations of the "dominion over the earth" (cf. Genesis) that the modern Western world has put forth through that which Jürgen Habermas calls instrumental reasoning. We find these, for example, in the Book of Job, whose author affirms that it is not the human being but rather God's gratuitous love that is the center and reason of all that is created. A theology of creation and of life can give much oxygen to the struggle for justice by widening its horizons.[37] Here we have a task that without doubt provides fertile ground for theological reflection on liberation.

This task will make us more sensitive to the aesthetic dimensions of the integral process of liberation, and because of this it must take into consideration all aspects of the human being. The right to beauty is an expression—and in many ways an urgent one—of the right to life. Human beings are subject to needs, but also to desires, and in this the postmodernists are correct. Our corporal dimension connects us in a special way to the natural world. It is a fountain of joy, the gift of life, but it is also a cry of the body of the poor, often in pain and hunger, as they anxiously await "the revealing of the children of God," as Paul says in a lovely and somewhat mysterious text (Rom. 8:19).

Theology faces a very important task: to deepen faith in a God, not out of fear but, as Albert Camus says, in a God "who laughs with humankind in the warm games of the sea and the sun." A God of life and joy.

Between Mysticism and Solidarity

Our current times make us see the urgency of something that can at first appear to be very basic: to give meaning to human existence. Different factors that have been noted in this article give reasons why many people today, especially young people, cannot see a reason for living. Without this, among other things, the struggle for a more just social order and for human solidarity would lose energy and lack any real force.

A critical task of the gospel message today is to contribute to giving meaning to life. Perhaps in the early days of theological work in Latin America we assumed it, as we also considered it as something that is inherently part of the inspiration of faith and the affirmation of fundamental truths of the Christian message. In any case, what is certain is that at the present time it is necessary to become concerned about the foundations of the human condition and the life of faith.

Again, it seems that commitment with the poor, inasmuch as this option centers in God's gratuitous love, has an important word to say about this matter. A tension is maintained between mysticism and historical solidarity, alluded to earlier. It is but one way, perhaps somewhat abstract, of repeating what the Gospel says with utter simplicity: the love of God and the love of neighbor is the sum of Jesus' message.

This is what really matters. I have to confess that I am less preoccupied with the interest or the survival of liberation theology than with the suffering and hopes of the people to whom I belong, and especially with the communication of the experience and the message of salvation in Jesus Christ. The latter is the substance of our love and our faith. A theology, no matter how relevant, is nothing but a medium for deepening those things. Theology is a hermeneutic of hope that is lived as a gift of God. In effect, that is what it means to proclaim liberating hope to the world in which we live today as church.

Translated by Isabel N. Docampo and Fernando Santillana

JOERG RIEGER

8. Developing a Common Interest Theology from the Underside

Contextual Theology and Special Interest Theology

At a time when liberation theologies all over the globe will soon be celebrating their thirtieth anniversaries, a comment by Frederick Herzog still rings true: Liberation theology, he pointed out, "appeared at a time of theological fads and was expected to last not much longer than a flash in the pan, similar to the death-of-God theology. Liberation theology was supposed to disappear fast. It did not."[1] As the global situation changes rapidly, we need to take another look for ourselves. Where is liberation theology now, and where are we going?

One of the major achievements of the theologies of liberation was a new awareness of the relation of theological thought and Christian praxis, a theme now echoed throughout the field.[2] Yet there is another, even more crucial question: Once theology descends from the ivory towers, where does it turn? Does not a theology which leaves the irrelevance of the ivory towers, at least in North America, automatically become a function of whatever context is closest to home, what some have been calling "contextual theology" or "genitive theology"? How can post-ivory-tower theology resist the market of ideas and contexts which, especially after the victory of capitalism with the fall of the Berlin Wall, appears to be spinning ever faster and faster?

I seriously wonder whether one of the reasons why liberation theology has been (and still is) misunderstood in the "First World"[3] has to do with the fact that it has been too closely identified with the idea of contextual theology. It is not only my first-year seminary students who keep confusing liberal and liberation theologies. For a while at least, modern liberal Protestantism seemed to be fascinated by what it saw as its own mirror image in the writings of those concerned about the underside of history, especially in other parts of the world.[4]

One of the troubles of this misunderstanding is, of course, that if the theologies of liberation are seen as simply another mode of modern liberal theology, they become passé by default once postmodernity rolls around. Quite a few theologians have tried to get rid of the challenge of liberation in this way. But that's the smaller problem. The real problem, especially in the First World, is that the identification of liberation theology and contextual theology has led people to perceive liberation theologies as "special interest theologies." The language of "advocacy scholarship" has at times contributed to the confusion. Liberation theologies thus are seen as ministering mainly to the interest of specific groups of different ethnic, gender, or class origins. This view gives permission for the rest of theology to go on with business as usual. How popular a misunderstanding this is can easily be seen, for instance, in class enrollment. Courses in Black Theology and the Black Church are usually attended either by African American students or by others who have some "special interest" in this type of thing. The same is true for the course on Hispanic theology that one of my colleagues started to teach recently.

Worse yet, if liberation theologians themselves happen to be pulled into these misunderstandings, it becomes difficult to identify what holds the various and often rather diverse strands of liberation theology together. In this case, liberation theology itself would become part of the market of ideas or competing contexts, withering away into postmodern difference.

Obviously, pluralistic fragmentation has not always been a problem for theologies trying to take matters of context seriously. Early contextual theologies were firmly anchored in universal anthropologies. The monolithic view of the present in the thought of Rudolf Bultmann and others was still able to identify common foundations and starting points.[5] Even the master of the method of correlation, Paul Tillich, could give a concise summary of what he saw as the general marks of human existence, namely a universal estrangement manifest in finitude, anxiety, and guilt.[6] Those "contextual" theologies could still fantasize about their relevance to universal humanity, which supposedly shared in a more or less common predicament.

Liberation theologies, on the other hand, have called for an awareness of social location in a much more radical sense. A monolithic view of the present was no longer viable due to the experience of real-life differences and suffering. Those at the margins soon began to understand that not all contexts are ultimately equal. The universals and foundations of modern theology were called into question, not primarily for philosophical reasons but because they neglected to take into account the plight of people at the margins. In this way, liberation theologies deconstructed the fundamental presuppositions of modern liberal theology, often before other contemporary critics, like the postmodern ones, made their appearance on the theological map.

Early on there were few paradigms available to grasp the new challenge. According to the existing ones, liberation theology could only be understood as a yet more radical contextual theology. What is surprising, however, is that even today many interpreters still feel that liberation theology has simply taken modern contextual theology, like the work of Bultmann and others, to its logical conclusion.[7] Opponents of liberation theology, on the other hand, still see this as an attack on "social unity,"[8] as if liberation theologians had destroyed a previously existing social harmony. This view feeds right into the widespread misunderstanding that the preferential option for the poor, apparently just another special interest claim, means that the gospel has nothing to say for the rich. In this paradigm, liberation theology can only be understood as special interest theology, relevant exclusively to people of the same group, with the possible exception of their benefactors.

I suspect that this categorization is one of the main reasons for the paradox that mainline theology felt on the one hand that it knew exactly what liberation theology was all about yet, on the other, had so much trouble dealing with it in any constructive way and learning anything from it. Liberation theology, understood as yet another contextual theology, could only lead to either disinterest (if this simply wasn't your own context) or to benevolent flights into the ghettoes or the Third World (if you happened to like what you read). By the same token, those who rejected contextual theologies altogether, felt they had to reject liberation theology even more.

One of the few theologians who understood early on that these paradigms were no longer helpful was Frederick Herzog. Already in 1974 he proposed a new vision, talking about liberation theologies as "common interest theologies."[9] Liberation theologies are not special interest theologies but address the common good from new angles, which now include the underside of history and a new vision of God. Liberation theologies are not in the business of pushing the concerns of certain groups over others. The point is to understand the *common* predicament in which both the marginalized and those in power share, without neglecting the obvious differences. Herzog reminds us of Paul's well-known dictum in 1 Cor. 12:26 that if one member suffers, all suffer together.[10] This means that unlike the various perspectives of privilege which feel they can afford to tend to their own context (the elite positions of the eye, the ear, the head, to stay with the image of the body), the view from the underside of suffering always reflects the whole body. Suffering can ultimately not be limited to one member only. Liberation theologies thus search for the best interest of all, seeking the liberating of both oppressors and oppressed by paying attention to where the pain is greatest. If this is seen, the rest of theology can no longer continue with business as usual. All of theology needs to join in listening to the common pain.

Liberation theologies have been clear about this point.[11] But I wonder if that point has ever been understood clearly enough in the reception of liberation approaches in the First World. If we are to escape the fate of other contextual theologies at the end of modernity and to resist the fluctuations of the market of ideas, that's precisely the point that we need to hammer out further. Facing the twenty-first century, we need to deepen some of liberation theology's main insights.

Which Context?

First of all, liberation theologians need to clarify further what is implied when we refer to matters of "context." Where do we turn once we have left the ivory towers? This clarification is necessary not only for those who are still not clear what liberation theology is all about. Time and again we also need this clarification from within.

Contextual theologies often proceed as if the context were already clear. To make theology contextual, in this model, means to relate it first of all to what concerns me or other people like myself. This is how the old advice to proceed with the Bible in the one hand and the newspaper in the other is often understood. After a certain amount of introspection of myself or my peer group, theology can run its course. Concern for others is not necessarily excluded, but this often tends to become a function of the concern for oneself. At Southern Methodist University, for instance, volunteer service has joined forces with the university's wellness program. The claim is that helping others is good for you. Starting from the perspective of oneself also means that we often feel that we are in a position to judge what the other needs and that we are able to fulfill that need. By telling ourselves and our children that the others are "just like us," we "look at someone who is different from us and come right back to ourselves."[12] This is how contextual theology is often practiced on the level of well-to-do middle-class churches across much of the conservative-liberal spectrum. In this model our own concerns, initiatives, and questions set the stage for theology, a serious self-evaluation is not necessary or might even be hurtful. According to Bultmann, one's existential relation to the world can only be ruined by too much reflection.[13]

This has not much to do with the dynamic that created the theologies of liberation. The concern for the "underside of history" is located at a different level. "Context" is not necessarily what is immediately obvious or closest to home. The context that matters most is not first of all our own but God's context, God's presence with those who need help the most. Does not God show a special concern for the one lost sheep, the sick, the poor, the widow, the orphan, the stranger, in short, for all those who suffer at the underside of history? Yet the true nature of the contextual reality of the underside is not immediately self-evident, surprisingly not even to those who live there. It takes some effort to cut through the covers and to understand. Gustavo Gutiérrez insists with good reason that "even the poor must make the option for the poor (I know many poor persons making the option to be rich)."[14] Dealing with the underside of history implies entering a different world. This world does not necessarily have to be far away. It is simply invisible to most of us. When at Southern Methodist University's Perkins School of Theology some students and faculty first became involved in West Dallas, a poor and heavily marginalized part of town only a few miles from campus, many of us felt we had entered a different world that most of us did not even know existed.

At the verge of enormous global transformations, we need to keep in mind that it is not always obvious what the appropriate context is to which liberation theology is related. A rule of thumb might be that context is that which hurts. This context, and this is the most crucial point, is not limited to those at the margins: it is also part of the (mostly repressed) reality of those who are part of the powers that be. Liberation theology is common interest theology, identifying common pain and seeking the liberation of both the poor and the rich, oppressed and oppressors.

Here is one of the hardest lessons to be learned yet, especially for those of us privileged ones who identify with liberation theology. Entering the world of the other will change the way we look at ourselves and our own context. Osmundo Afonso Miranda has observed the problem well: "Some North American liberation theologians speak more or less like the liberals of the last century and advocate partial liberation of the oppressed as long as it does not curtail their own fringe benefits derived from exploitation."[15] In the encounter with real pain there can be no easy alliance with liberation theology any more.

Liberation theology, no matter of which provenience, is a theology which knows that the other is part of our context. In the words of the apostle Paul, the eye cannot say to the hand, "I have no need of you." (1 Cor. 12:21) Here is one of the biggest differences between contextual theology and liberation theology. In taking another look at the underside of history, liberation theology starts to notice certain aspects of reality that contextual theology will never see. This does not mean that contextual theology is completely unaware of suffering, pain, and structures of oppression. But contextual theology tends to see those structures as exceptions, anomalies, merely deviations from the normal course of things. Liberation theology, on the other hand, understands that suffering, pain, and oppression are not merely accidental but point to a deeper truth about the dominant contexts. Conflicts and tensions do not appear out of nowhere but are produced by the prevailing system itself, and as such point to its unconscious truth, which the powers that be must constantly repress in order to preserve the way things are. As Walter

Benjamin, a German thinker of Jewish descent and a victim of the Third Reich, realized, it is exactly "the tradition of the oppressed" that "teaches us that the 'state of emergency' in which we live is not the exception but the rule."[16] Consequently, it is in identification with the suffering other that one finds the truth about oneself and the key to understanding the mechanisms of the system of which one is a part.

While contextual theology has developed few tools to read between the lines of the context, liberation theologies have done a much better job. Nevertheless, we still need better theological and other tools. An observation of Frederick Herzog in the late 1980s remains true, especially in the First World, namely that "there is little understanding thus far that exactly in regard to scholarship the poor of the world are calling Western Christianity to account."[17] We need a better understanding not only of those at the underside of history but also of those who put them there. Already Martin Luther King Jr. had made a similar observation in the context of the Civil Rights Movement. While there are many studies on the damage of racism to African Americans, we still lack a sense of its corrosive effects on whites. Over thirty years later, most of us still have not done our homework.[18]

At the turn of the century, liberation theologies need to add more layers to their current understanding of context in terms of the underside of history. How would my self-understanding as a middle-class Western, white male change, for instance? The point is not to increase the guilty feelings of liberal minds but to get a grasp of the web of relationships that is already in place. At the same time more voices from the underside are making themselves heard. Lately, Hispanic theology for instance has reminded us that the struggle for liberation is yet more complex, arguing that our reflections need to include the aspects of culture and identity as well. Womanist theology, to name another major perspective which has emerged in recent years, has begun to raise questions about the status of women who are African American and poor. The reality of those who suffer from triple oppression contributes to deepen the awareness of suffering and oppression, reminding us that there is no easy way out of the current system. *Mujerista* theology is yet another voice that reminds us of the various intersections of oppression.[19]

Recently, some theologians have again argued for the need to pay attention not only to the official texts and doctrines of the church but also to the discourse of ordinary Christians, especially those to whom theology has not yet listened.[20] The work of Mary McClintock Fulkerson, a feminist theologian, may serve as an example. Fulkerson has developed a framework of analysis which contributes to a new awareness of the context of women who have not yet been accounted for by feminist theology: Her work with lower-class Pentecostal women of the Appalachian mountains, for instance, helps to expand further the horizons of liberation theology. "Changing the Subject," so the title of her book, is an ongoing task, even for liberation theologians. Fulkerson reminds us, furthermore, that we need to pay closer attention to structures of oppression. First World Christians, used to being in control, often forget that personal efforts of good will, or personal confessions of failure, are not enough. In Fulkerson's words: "Simply to confess historicality and transitoriness is not enough. Nor are authorial confessions of social location sufficient, since the individual consciousness is not the (sole) source of oppressive formations."[21] We need a more specific account of actual suffering and its causes.

Liberation theology, particularly in the First World, needs to deepen its understanding of structural injustice. Not because the personal is not important but because our understanding of structures is still underdeveloped. As far as structural injustice is concerned, over the last thirty years race and gender have slowly started to surface in the consciousness of the North American public. No doubt, there is a lot left to be done in these areas, and some recent developments such as the challenge to affirmative action in California and elsewhere show how glaring is our lack of understanding of structures. But it seems to me that we are even further behind in matters of class and economic injustice. If the Disney Company is any indication for contemporary trends and attitudes, their recent movie *Pocahontas* might illustrate the situation. This movie is about an encounter between the female hero, a Native American woman, and a young white explorer from England. This explorer learns that the Native Americans are not savages, that they have their own culture, and that the Native American woman with whom he falls in love will not give up her life in order to follow him back to London where he needs to return for medical treatment. While gender, culture, and race differences are addressed to some degree in this movie, there is no awareness of class. The en-

counter between Pocahontas and John Smith takes place on the
upper and enlightened levels of society, she is the daughter of the
local Indian Chief and he is the captain of the British ship. Yet
everyday encounters are hardly ever limited to the level of gender and race.

Economic disparities are an increasingly important part of
the picture even though they seem to be far less conscious. This
is one of the major challenges which extends to theology as well.
At a time when the market has finally become God,[22] how seriously does contemporary theology, liberation theology included,
address economic issues? This question is becoming ever more
central. While the Protestant Reformers of the sixteenth century still dealt with a human being that was primarily religious,
the Enlightenment deals with the political human being. Today,
however, while much of First World theology is still caught up
with the *homo politicus'* dream of autonomy and control, the
globalizing world of the twenty-first century is moving on to the
human being as an economic animal, *homo oeconomicus.*[23]
Whether we like it or not, economic relationships now determine
much of our lives.

There is a certain postmodern ring to some of these insights
which may lead to another misunderstanding: The point is not a
further fragmentation of experience and context, *ad infinitum*, as
it were. The point is a more perceptive account of the multifac-
eted realities at the underside of history which permits a better
view of the common predicament of the "body," which is now
global. This is the major issue that distinguishes liberation theology from contextual theology, even of the latest postmodern
brands. Liberation theology is not interested in piling up more
special interest theologies. Neither is it promoting pluralism for
its own sake. [24]

The challenge for liberation theology in the twenty-first century is this: We must learn how to devise more specific analyses
of context on the one hand while not losing sight of the overar-
ching concern for the underside of history on the other. We need
to keep together more specific accounts of the diversity and complexity of human life and an understanding of the common roots
of suffering. The possibility of further collaboration will depend
on it.

Of course, these reflections do not exhaust liberation theology's
concern for the underside of history. In recent years it has become

clear that the look from the underside of history is by no means only an analytical one. It can also spark new hope. As Gustavo Gutiérrez has pointed out, in the life of the poor joy and hope transpire as well.[25] Here lie as-yet-untapped powers of transformation. Mary McClintock Fulkerson's encounter with the plight of poor Appalachian women, for instance, leads to an encouraging understanding of the transforming power of God's presence in unexpected places.

Where Is God?

In North America the myth still persists in some places that liberation theology is all about ethics or right action, orthopraxis. What this view fails to recognize, however, is that a more fundamental interest of liberation theology lies in the doctrine of God. Any orthopraxis is ultimately related to God's own praxis, which precedes all human action. At least in the First World, still largely defined by the structures of white male success, calls for social action are most likely merely to perpetuate the power of the establishment without changing much in the lives of the disenfranchised. One of the major tasks for liberation theology is the further development of its understanding of God's work.

As Gustavo Gutiérrez and others have pointed out, liberation theology approaches the question of God from a different angle. For the past 200 years mainline First World theology has been preoccupied with the question of the existence of God. While this question is becoming less important even in First World theology, this has never been the primary question for people who suffer. The question for many of the oppressed, not only in Latin America, is not whether there is a God but where is God?[26] This question arises not out of theological curiosity but out of the need to be close to God. This is one of the most important questions arising at the underside of history that liberation theology has picked up.

Leaving the theological ivory towers, thinking as living beings rather than as disembodied thinkers, is therefore not the only thing that we need to worry about. We need to explore further where God is in all of this. Modern contextual theologies proceeded under the assumption that God is everywhere, which has often been taken to mean that God is on our side. Yet this will no longer do. We need to ask again, where is God?

In the First World context there is a long history of the modern self which has had little trouble imagining that God is always on its side. Growing up in Germany, I once found a belt-buckle in our garage which one of my grandfathers seems to have worn as a German soldier in World War II and which read, *Gott mit uns,* "God with us." In North America, the doctrine of Manifest Destiny has assured us for a long time that God is on our side, no matter what. Even in the 1990s many Americans did not have to think long about praying that God might bless our troops in the Gulf War; in fact I do not recall much soul-searching about whether God wanted us to go to Kuwait in the first place. But even apart from these grand schemes, on the level of everyday life, the modern assurance that God is on our side has invaded much of what is going on in our churches. In most places the question, Where is God? is hardly ever raised in a serious fashion. We just know intuitively that "he" is on our side.

For this reason the use of notions like "orthopraxis" can easily backfire in the North American context. The focus on the right praxis of those in power, based on concepts of autonomy and superiority, seems to reinforce a certain myopia which is unable to acknowledge the other, except as recipient of charity. Yet the encounter with the human other and the divine Other always go hand in hand, as liberation theology reminds us. If we miss the human other, we might have trouble encountering the divine Other. In light of the encounter with the other, we need to take another look at where God is at work in the present. This is why Frederick Herzog talked about God-walk, Christopraxis,[26] and Spirit-praxis, rather than about orthopraxis. The contextual reality that he was searching for was not first of all our own but God's and the other's. One of the most important questions at present is therefore not, what else can we do? but, what is Jesus doing now?

Herzog never stopped reminding us that liberation theology must always be clear about who is doing the liberating in the first place. Only then can special interest theology gradually become common interest theology, without having to sacrifice differences. Only if God is the liberator will liberation affect all of humanity, although not always in the same way. The parable of the Prodigal Son in the Gospel of Luke, chapter 15, talks about God's relation to two very different sons. As a result, First World Christians in touch with the powers that be might find that, while God may not have abandoned us yet, God is not automatically on our side in the ways we had assumed.

For liberation theology, an important part of the answer to the question, where is God? is God's own involvement with the oppressed, a vision supported throughout God's history with ancient Israel, the church, and particularly in the life of Christ. Liberation theology knows that any preferential option for the poor can only be God's own option. The option for the poor has nothing to do with any privileges that the poor would own. The concern for the underside of history is not based on the essential qualities of the poor but relates to God's praxis with the poor throughout the centuries. Liberation theology does not continue liberal theology's foundationalism.

Liberation theology is not one more special interest theology built upon the claim that the poor now own God, no matter what. While there is always the danger that those who are used to being in control will appropriate God and Christ for their own purposes, things look somewhat different at the underside of history. In one of his last articles Herzog has rendered this more explicit. He reminds us that "God will not be seen where the divine can be controlled." Here the poor introduce a different perspective. "The poor, as such, do not demonstrate God, and yet they are the place for us to 'see' God. How can this be?" A partial answer to this fundamental question has to do with the fact that "the poor cannot be controlled."[28] A new window into the work of God opens up in unexpected ways. A common interest theology must allow for a new encounter with God beyond the control of the powers that be. Confronted with the question, where is God? we must realize that God's presence in Christ can no longer be controlled.

This sheds some light on a major problem in the reception of liberation theology in First World theology which I suspect reflects the main camps of theology today. It seems to me that often the preferential option for the poor is either taken to mean that the poor now assume the prominent place of authority and control that has been occupied by the modern self in much of modern theology, or that the poor simply become the central focus of charity and well-meaning support from those who are better off. Either the poor control theology and thus God, or they have nothing to contribute to theology at all. Yet both extremes miss the point since they fail to take seriously both God and the poor. Putting the poor in the place of ultimate authority would not only limit God's authority but also misunderstand the actual situation of the poor. Any foundationalism built on the oppressed will simply end up romanticizing them! Making the poor into recipients of charity, on the other hand, does of course not take them seriously either. Worse yet, this would also fail to take seriously God, who freely identifies with the "least of these" (Matthew 25). Mainline theology needs new paradigms if it wants to understand the role of the poor in theology.[29]

Liberation theology grows, thus, out of a double encounter. Two moments are tied together: the eruption of the marginalized from the underside of history on the one hand, and the irruption of God on the other. Liberation theology draws together the implications of the eruption of the people in history and God's irruption into history in the light of the gospel. Stronger than most other liberation theologians, Herzog, knowing firsthand about the temptations of a theology done by the privileged, has emphasized the aspect of God's irruption.[30] Herzog's concern is still key for a First World context where the specific shapes of God's irruption are often covered up by our own pious agendas and orthopraxes. As masters of contextual theology, we have a hard time understanding that the theological position of the marginalized might differ from the theological position of the autonomous modern self and its constant struggles for authority and control. In the First World, God's irruption reminds us of two moments that must come together in an encounter with the underside of history: our observation of how God is at work and our awareness that the modern self cannot control God. Only then can we hope to develop a spirituality that does not give up concrete historical questions in locating God's presence but is at the same time aware of the ongoing need for questioning and self-critique.

It seems to me that this approach creates room for the Holy Spirit, since liberation theology begins exactly at the point where we become aware of our own limitations in light of the encounter with the underside of history. Here the eruption of the marginalized teaches all of theology a valuable lesson. Paradoxically, at first sight, in this process the context can be taken more seriously since it no longer needs to serve as warrant for ultimate theological authority, which can only be in the hands of God. In fact, the same is true for the church's scriptures and traditions.

A Look Ahead

Liberation theology understands itself as common interest theology. For this reason it is not just the business of nontraditional sections of the academy or of those who are forced to live at the underside of history. While those are the places that gave rise to liberation theology, today no theology can afford not to give an account of what God is doing among those who suffer the most. The theologies of God's liberating work with those who suffer and those who (often unconsciously) inflict suffering, pose a major challenge to theology in general. The fact that most people belong to both camps in some way or another makes this challenge all the more real. In conclusion let me offer some impulses for theology as it continues into the twenty-first century.

Becoming New Theologians

When I mention to people that I am involved in the liberation theology project as white Western male with a German and North American theological background, I sometimes notice this blank look on their faces. If liberation theology is simply another contextual theology, this indeed does not make a lot of sense. Frederick Herzog was among the few theologians in a similar situation who blazed the trail. In response to another colleague who deals with liberation issues but does not feel entitled to call himself a liberation theologian because he does not belong to an oppressed group, he puts it this way: "Is it not rather the other way around, that theology needs to describe what God is doing in any group?"[31]

Even Western white male theologians need to understand that we are no longer free to pursue our own special interests. Upon entering the academy, too many of us still feel "like a kid in a candy store," as one of my colleagues put it to me recently. This is one of the major challenges for the twenty-first century. While not necessarily opposing the development of liberation theologies, we need to admit that we often have left liberation theology to those who hurt, not realizing that we, too, are involved in their stories. Already the apostle Paul understood that if one member hurts, all members of the body hurt. Liberation theology has taken a next step in reminding us that the pain is not coming out of nowhere and that we need to do a better job listening to the symptoms of suffering in order to understand our own role in the system.

How do white males come to join the liberation theology project? The encounter with the otherness of God must no longer be separated from the encounter with the human other. It will not happen merely at the level of ideas. When I entered seminary, my mother had just received her license as a local preacher in the German United Methodist Church. Although she did not have to suffer terrible injustices, observing the way she was received by the church, the places she was and was not sent to preach, was a first step in a long process that gradually opened my own eyes to the underside of history. I never looked at theology and the church in quite the same way again. In recent times my involvement in one of the most devastated neighborhoods of Dallas has brought me in contact with situations that I was only dimly aware existed in the First World on such a broad scale. I found once again that meeting God at the underside of history can change your life.

The new theologians will be "organic intellectuals." This notion of Antonio Gramsci has accompanied the development of liberation theology from the outset. Gramsci distinguishes between organic and traditional intellectuals. The difference between the two camps is not that one group is contextual while the other is not. The difference is that one group is not aware of its context while the other group is trying to gain greater clarity about it. The so-called traditional intellectuals, according to Gramsci, "put themselves forward as autonomous and independent."[32] They do not realize that they are in fact shaped by their own context. As a result, they often become functions of the *status quo* and end up preserving it. It is interesting that Gramsci found many of those intellectuals in the church. The organic intellectuals, on the other hand, include their context in their intellectual reflections. In this way they are forced to take into account their own biases. This is not only an analytical move but a constructive one as well: Organic intellectuals are led to put their intellectual capabilities to work for the improvement of real life.

Paradoxically, mainline contextual theology is often closer to the position of Gramsci's traditional intellectuals than to that of the organic intellectuals since one's own context is presupposed but not further examined. First World contextual theology thus often ends up as celebration of its own context. There is not much room for God's praxis at the underside of history which at times challenges and calls into question our social locations. Organic intellectuals, by contrast, seek to reduce the constant temptation to render their own context absolute. In relating to a different context, the context of those at the grassroots, self-critical reflection becomes possible. In this process, the primary task for organic *theologians* is to learn again how to listen and to find out to whom to listen.

On this backdrop the words of an Australian Aboriginal woman to a person of good will make sense: "If you're coming to help me, you are wasting your time. But if you have come because your liberation is bound up with mine, then let us work together."[33] Liberation theologians are not those who save the world by their own actions. Liberation theologians are those who are aware that their own actions need to be constantly transformed by God's liberation, which sets free the oppressors as well as the oppressed.

Toward a Common Tradition

The search for context always starts at home. One of the theologians most concerned about things on a local level that I have ever met was Frederick Herzog. At the same time he understood that liberation theology is not special interest theology. In his last years he became increasingly involved in struggles for liberation on a global scale. He saw the need to uncover what he called the "common tradition" of the Americas and Europe, which is first of all a common tradition of violence that produced the death of 100 million Indians from Hispaniola to Wounded Knee.[34] Herzog became more and more convinced that "the vast masses of the poor and the destruction of the environment on both continents have become an all-encompassing challenge for our interpretation of the Bible, of the whole Christian tradition, and of our modern human selfhood."[35] While he was not able to continue this work, this is the continuing challenge for liberation theology in the twenty-first century.

Herzog's example reminds us that this common tradition must not be based on a romantic idea. There is no use in harking back to the universal starting points of early contextual theology. What ties North and South together is not first of all a common essence, common tastes, or a common history of ideas, but the reality of massive suffering at the hands of European immigrants that has never been fully accounted for. Like common interest theology, the common tradition grows out of an account of the suffering of humanity and creation that often goes unnoticed. Such an understanding of a common tradition does not impose uniformity but will allow for a listening to diverse voices of pain.

One of the prime challenges for the theologies of liberation at the turn of the century is to continue to develop better understandings of *common structures* of oppression. The different modes of liberation theology need to become even more aware of the links that are already in place at the underside of history. Real solidarity can only grow where it becomes clear that the whole body suffers together. It is from this perspective that we then can address global structures of power, like the globalization of the economy which has so rapidly advanced in recent years.

The search for a common tradition does not end in the analytical mode. Practical solidarity leads to new relationships. To the common history of oppression corresponds a common history of liberation. In this process, liberation theologians hit upon new models for ecumenical relationships among Christians of different denominations.[36] Not even in the church can a common tradition be built from the top down any more, starting with conversations on the level of ideas and ending by issuing appeals to the people in the pews. A common tradition emerges where relationships are built at the grassroots, where people join in God's work. The pressures of a global economy are bringing those who are left out closer together.

At the same time, neither a common tradition nor a common interest theology must do away with the different identities of the participants. One of the lessons learned in the Civil Rights struggle is that the idea of the "melting pot" is an illusion. The point is not to make everybody into one image, which is usually the image of the powerful anyway, but to value and acknowledge difference. Herzog suggests a model: "The goal is to weave the separate histories into one history in which the single strands do not lose their original color."[37] The main objective of the search for a common tradition is not the creation of a single identity in which everything becomes alike but a fresh encounter with the plight of the other. In this process the First World can finally learn from the Third World, those in power can finally learn from those at the margins, men from women, whites from blacks, the rich from the poor, and so on. Mainline theology is now provided a mirror in the encounter with liberation theology.

Still, the reconstruction and further development of a common tradition is a most sensitive issue, for any interaction will need to keep in mind the existing asymmetry between those at the margins and those who are in control. All attempts initiated by those in power that seek to "liberate" the oppressed, rather than to first examine their own position in the mirror-image of the other self-critically, are highly problematic. Common interest theology can only be developed further when all begin to share in God's own concern for the widow, the orphan, and the stranger, the "least of these" who cross our path every day.

FREDERICK HERZOG

9. New Birth of Conscience

"What is our blindness today?" Theology moves forward when great questions arise. This one, posed by George E. Tinker, an Osage/Cherokee, will haunt us far into the twenty-first century. Tinker earlier had referred to what Christian missions have done to native peoples of South and North America by wanting to "do good," moving them into "reductions" or "reservations," while simultaneously robbing them of their cultural values and their way of life. "With the best of intentions, and with the full support of our best theologies and intellectual capabilities, do we continue to fall into the same sorts of traps and participate in unintended evils?" If this is the question haunting us, Tinker is very clear about its presupposition: "Without confronting and owning our past, as white Americans, as Europeans, as American Indians, as African Americans, and so forth, we cannot hope to overcome that past and generate a constructive healing process, leading to a world of genuine, mutual respect among peoples, communities, and nations."[1]

At the moment, some theologians are ringing their hands about the "death" of theology. What is happening to theology has been brought home by William C. Placher: "Theology has a bad reputation in most Christian churches these days—it's regarded as obscure, hard to understand, irrelevant, a bit of a joke."[2] What is theology's blindness? For lack of interest in theology, theologians themselves are partly to blame. In our capitalist society, theology too has often become private enterprise. As one theologian recently told me when I asked for whom he was writing theology: "For myself."

In an unsuspecting moment, there was Oklahoma City: the bomb heard around the world. Arab terrorists invading our shores? No, Americans killing Americans, especially children. The vast violence has been there all along in our country, but now it jolts us into common accountability. Where did we go wrong?

In our American tradition, there have been moments of radical awakening from comatose states. One such moment was when Abraham Lincoln, in the midst of the Civil War, with the emancipation of the slaves on his mind, tried to appeal to the creativity of the American people: "The dogmas of the quiet past, are inadequate to the stormy present. The occasion is piled high with difficulty, and we must rise with the occasion. As our case is new, so we must think anew, and act anew. We must disenthrall ourselves" (December 1, 1862).[3]

Also in our day, the dogmas of the quiet past are no longer adequate to the stormy present. What happened in Lincoln's day obviously was very violent. For our day, we have to create a nonviolent history, and we have to read the past critically. Recently, Swiss theologian Walter J. Hollenweger tried to sum up the "difficulty piled high" in much of the theological heritage we received from Europe: "Scholarly theology is bankrupt not because its products are completely worthless, but because it cannot transport its products to where they are more needed than the daily bread, that is, to church and society."[4] In parts of Protestantism, transporting our products to church and society has been a theological compulsion for the past two hundred years. Much North American Protestant theology has promoted the apologetic notion that it has to adjust itself to the "man come of age." In an inverted sense, Protestant missions often have not done things very differently, for example, in Latin America, as they tried to cater to the economic ambitions of explorers, pioneers, and entrepreneurs.

Hollenweger suggests, as a way out, renewal through a narrative theology close to the Bible, and he compares the theologian's job with that of a car manufacturer who, in the process of designing the car, always keeps the buyer in mind.[5] This does not help, however, in view of the Oklahoma City bomb. Our unique North American challenge is not primarily a hermeneutic one: to communicate the gospel to church and society. Our mandate is to become the *theological detective,* to discover the basic flaw in the history of the American church and society: the contempt for the dignity of the Indian, the black, and the woman. We have "known" this for some time. But our primal flaw, the genocide of the Indian, has hardly been explored theologically together with American Indians. I suspect this repression keeps us from seeing our present flaw: our continuing domination of those who are weak.

With today's situation also "piled high with difficulty," we can "rise with the occasion." We had thought at times that we had solved at least a few of society's problems. Oklahoma City woke us up to the fact that the terrorists were "patriotic" Americans who, in an atmosphere fostered also by ultraright Christians, were killing other Americans at random. Now we need to do even more theological detective work. Western Christianity has a long history of "patriotic" violence since the days of Constantine and, on our shores, since the Spanish Conquest. From Columbus on Hispaniola in 1492 to Wounded Knee in 1890, the "patriotic" cruelties done to Indians by well-meaning Christians are mind boggling. As an Indian witness, American Horse, described the scene at Wounded Knee, fleeing mothers with their children were "shot right through," including those who were pregnant or nursing.[6] L. Frank Baum, author of the *Wizard of Oz*, as editor of the *Aberdeen Saturday Pioneer*, dared to write: "The Whites, by law of conquest, by justice of civilization, are masters of the American continent, and the best safety of the frontier settlements will be secured by the total annihilation of the few remaining Indians."[7]

Historian David E. Stannard and others figure there might have been 100 million Indian dead from Hispaniola to Wounded Knee.[8] Add the brutal story of six million blacks dying on the "passage." While these events seem long past, they force us to detect our present blindness—which brings us to our sweet advantages of life in the "rich" nations today derived from the exploitation of poor nations, involving a war by other means:

> The third world war has already started. It is a silent war. Not, for that reason, any less sinister. This war is tearing down Brazil, Latin America and practically all the Third World. Instead of soldiers dying, there are children. It is a war over the Third World debt, and which has as its main weapon interest, a weapon more deadly than the atom bomb, more shattering than a laser beam. (Luiz Ignacio Lula da Silva, head of Brazil's Workers' Party)

The hidden terror of this war also reaches into our cities and Indian reservations, where poverty is worse than a decade ago. Our continuing complicity in the domination over other people in our own country is focused in the Indian reservation. What kind of christology do we operate with as people who sustain the Indian reservation? Our habit of the heart is violent. Nonviolence involves the Sisyphean task of shaping an alternate society or "reinventing" America.

So "our case is new" (Lincoln). With the event of Oklahoma City, we are under the gun of our gun culture. Had we realized what violence we, as one of the world's top weapons dealers, inflict upon ourselves? It is not just the weight of what President Eisenhower called the military-industrial complex but also the cultural violence in every nook and cranny of society: battering of women, rape, child abuse, and the violence of movies and TV. Will we theologians immersed in such violence share in God's own walk into the turmoil of our violent history? Abandoning a theology of private self-consciousness, "God-walk" would be the fusion of our bodies with our words, and truth would be that for which we put our life on the line.

"What is our blindness today?" We do not as yet detect how deeply we are caught in the mass psychology of violence that antecedes the two World Wars and goes back at least to 1492 and the subsequent Conquest. It is ingeniously disguised. Just like slavery and segregation, the reservation has not as yet entered the ken of our theologies as starting point and mold of our doctrinal deconstruction and construction. Yet in the midst of disguise, we cannot but detect also the nonviolent hope, the life-affirming dream of our history.

So we need a new primer of what it means to be human. "Thinking anew and acting anew" (Lincoln) today means for a while to hold back reproducing the creed with its doctrines of God, Christ, Holy Spirit, and church. Dogmas are part of our past. We can interpret them. I have done this for more than four decades. Right now, we have to face ourselves in the mirror and learn how the violence we as human beings bring to dogma shapes its use—at times brutally. We need a transformation of our superiority madness and its implicit power wielding. We need a new birth of conscience.

The first step for me is to continue facing the truth of Auschwitz and linking it to other Christian inflictions of death. For half a century, we tried to understand how the Holocaust could have happened among "Christianized" German people. Among many others, Sidney G. Hall, in *Christian Anti-Semitism and Paul's Theology*, calls for a theology that "evolves out of Auschwitz."[9] When theologians claimed that Jesus was the *only* child of God for all humanity, not just *a* child of God embodying God's invitation to all, it paved the way for intolerance: Everyone who was not a Christian had to become a Christian. Paul, rather, seems to contend, Hall claims, that Jews could accept the gospel of Christ without becoming "Christian."[10] Since God's work in Christ results in the liberation of nonpersons, the church is moving toward an inclusive theology "out of the cries of dead Jewish children."[11]

Hall calls attention to the tragic error: Christians assuming they have a better faith than Jews. Yet are not we theologians still blind to a further feeling of superiority? In reviewing Judaism, Christianity, and liberation theology, Hall claims he could not call his theology a liberation theology because he does not belong to an oppressed group.[12] Is it not rather the other way around: that theology needs to describe what God is doing in any group? "God-walk" will not allow theologians to determine beforehand where God's liberation can or cannot take place.

Hall quotes Dietrich Bonhoeffer about the need "to see the great events of world history from below," the place of the underdog.[13] As we walk on this land, we need to look below our feet, where lie buried the bones of Native Americans whom we forced to die before their time. To break the spell of present-day theology, we can begin with reflecting on God's walk among the Indians. It involves a *transvaluation of our values of superiority.* God puts pressure on human conscience to evoke value change. When we lose the last vestige of superiority feelings over those who owned the land, we are weak, yet therefore strong (2 Cor. 12:10).

In our weakness, we find ourselves theologically between postmodern theology, with a great variety of religious sensibility, and a nonfoundational theology, practically denying variety as foundation of theology. Terrence Tilley, together with various coauthors, has given us an excellent overview of the former stance in *Postmodern Theologies: The Challenge of Religious Diversity.*[14] One tacit—and occasionally not so tacit—assumption here is Christianity's need to be in solidarity with other religions. But how are we to understand this solidarity? Tilley speaks, on the one hand, of postmodern approaches emphasizing a reductive pluralism of *religious* traditions and, on the other hand, of approaches that stress irreducible particularities while nevertheless aspiring to inclusivity or even universalism of *religion*.

Theological postmodernism here presses toward a universal category of *religion*. Yet Jesus did not appeal to some "religious otherness" (apparently a major postmodern reference to God) but to God's walk among the suffering. Instead of *universality*, Jesus in his walk embodies the *protection privilege of the poor*. He invites us concretely to commit ourselves to others in distress. That pertains to Wounded Knee and hundreds of other places of the Conquest, including the auction blocks of black slaves and the abuse of women. Walking this road, we break the spell of fitting Jesus into the universal of religion.

Rejecting a Jesus subservient to any universal framework of religion is forcefully expressed in nonfoundationalism. The critique, for example, in *Theology without Foundations: Religious Practice and the Future of Theological Truth*, edited by Stanley Hauerwas, Nancey Murphy, and Mark Nation, is based on a reaction to Réne Descartes's assumption that modern thought had to rebuild the foundations of reason and to the later claim of theological liberalism that theology had to be raised again on this new foundation.[15]

While modernist and postmodernist frameworks are here left behind, some nonfoundationalists end up with an exclusive base in the church that borders on the doctrine of "outside the church there is no salvation." All important things theological happen within the confines of a kind of "Loveboat" church. Yet God's protection privilege of the poor often grabs people outside any "churchianity." The communal conscience of humanity is the place where Jesus today may be working most effectively. Instead of *churchianity*, God offers us *communal conscience*. St. Paul keenly detects this "umpire" of truth: "We appeal to every person's conscience before God" (2 Cor. 4:2).

Here lies the need for time out, for "disenthrallment" (Lincoln), a common effort at breaking the spell of superiority, universality, and churchianity. It calls for a radically different theology. We are called to mutuality in truth seeking that transcends individual theologies. We forget that the church did not begin with books about Jesus or religious talk, but with people walking with Jesus, sensing God's nearness in their communal conscience, and, later, breaking bread with each other, celebrating Jesus' presence. Being people of "the way" (Acts 9:2), their life was the art of listening together to communal conscience, a knowing together with God, *conscientia* in a corporate way. Present in this conscience is God's constant transvaluation of values in the protection privilege of the poor. Here *art unites, but religion divides.*

Vincent Van Gogh knew of a Jesus who is "the greatest artist of all, disdaining marble, clay or colour, working with living flesh . . . this unbelievable artist, one who is scarcely conceivable to such an obtuse instrument as the modern neurotic, wornout brain, made neither statues, nor pictures, nor books; indeed, he said clearly enough what he was doing—fashioning living men, immortal beings."[16]

We grasp Jesus' art by walking along with God among the Indian dead of yesterday and the culturally dead of today's Indian reservation. Vine Deloria Jr. observes: "Indians were encouraged to adopt the values and attitudes of the consumer society."[17] The best way to stop imposing our consumer values is to join God in resisting them. Forty-five percent of the potential Indian work force is unemployed. That compares "favorably" with the percentage of young blacks unemployed in the United States. Only if we change ourselves in view of these "invisible" people, will we become aware of the "invisible God." Here anchors our theological future. There is the modern brutalization thrust among Christian nations from the First through the Second World War until today, weighing heavily on our theological thought patterns. It all circles around the fiendish destructiveness of economics, of money, or mammon, increasingly ruling our lives more than God. Being freed from mammon's demonic power, we will excruciatingly learn, in Lincoln's words, "to think anew and act anew."

Secular analogies today prove that the art of peaceful revolution is becoming a viable option. The Berlin wall fell on account of the courage of countless conscience-bound people when nobody expected it. With Greenpeace appealing to the communal conscience of the world, neither government nor commercial "powers that be" could afford to have the *Brent Spar* hauled off to its ocean-polluting grave. Contemporary governments and transnational corporations can be compelled to let conscience-evoking groups cogovern without recourse to violence—toward an alternate society.

If we detect the true character of our North American social dilemma, we will discover that we are still accomplices of our

for us it's optional to be inclusive

society's war and violence machinery. Its metaphor, Oklahoma City, is a mandate for a weaponless society. In Tilley's postmodern book appears Edith Wyschogrod's moving story of the French Protestants of Chambon, people who rescued Jews during World War II. Her point is that the postmodern saintly life "is a plea for boldness and risk."[18] There are similar examples in nonfoundationalism. Stanley Hauerwas' stress on the Holocaust memory is an instance.[19] This is bedrock we cannot ever evade. Segregation had to go, but there is still the Indian reservation. We now need immense boldness not to continue forcing the Native American into the harsh choice between bingo palace and unemployment. We need to risk the protection privilege of the poor to resound in North American communal conscience, so any future theology will be compelled to take its starting point here: exegesis, church history, systematic as well as practical theology.

Thirty years after the first signs of black power appeared on the horizon and we could hear the distant thunder of black theology approaching, there is hardly an impact to be detected in the dominant Protestant theology. James Cone proves to be right: Blacks do not "exist" for us. We should not be surprised about the hue and cry over new racism. Theology is even less affected by Native American theology. What is needed is a basic revamping of all theology as we relate it to the "common tradition" of conquest-violence between South and North America, compelling us to shape theology with both continents in mind, demanding their equal due. This project will bring about a new christology and a new theological education. Yet first of all, we need time out for what Lincoln called "disenthrallment": a new birth of conscience.

So "in my soul" I kneel in the grass of the Dakota prairies that gave me birth. Today, knowing a little more of the "Trail of Tears" that led also through these prairies to Wounded Knee, I bury my head in the grass, incapable of tears. Looking up again, in my mind I see on the horizon toward the East the smoke of the ovens of Auschwitz. "Stony road we trod, bitter the chastening rod, felt in the days when hope unborn had died." In small compass, this is my life—gutted yet not burned out, with "miles to go before I sleep." God all along is walking against the tyranny of mammon, superiority, and power while reinventing the American— nonviolently. "No statement, theological or otherwise, should be made that would not be credible in the presence of burning children" (Irving Greenberg).[20]

Notes

Preface

1. Frederick Herzog, *God-Walk: Liberation Shaping Dogmatics* (Maryknoll, N.Y.: Orbis, 1988), xxii.
2. Frederick Herzog, "Theology of Liberation," *Continuum* 7:4 (Winter 1970); James H. Cone, *A Black Theology of Liberation* (Philadelphia and New York: Lippincott, 1970); Gustavo Gutiérrez, *Teología de la liberación: Perspectivas* (Lima: CEP, 1971); Rosemary Radford Ruether, *Liberation Theology* (New York: Paulist Press, 1972). Gutiérrez started to use the term *liberation theology* in a lecture in 1968.
3. James H. Cone, *God of the Oppressed* (Minneapolis: Seabury Press, 1975), 50, has acknowledged this by stating that to his knowledge "only one white theologian, Frederick Herzog in *Liberation Theology*, has attempted to reorder theological priorities in the light of the oppression of black people."

1. Introduction

1. While theology is often expanded to include matters of culture, critical reflection on issues of the economy is often not part of the picture. The *Christian Century's* summary of "top religious stories of 1997," for example, while mentioning the ethics of cloning and even welfare reform, included no reference to economic underpinnings. *The Christian Century* (January 7–14, 1998), 14–19. Thanks to Susan Thistlethwaite for suggesting the title of this Introduction.
2. This reference is left out of Gutiérrez's essay as included in this volume.
3. I use the designations First World and Third World with caution, since they are not unproblematic. I will keep them, however, because they remind us of actual relationships of political and economic power. The use of other terms like "one-third" and "two-thirds" world has the disadvantage of covering up the structures that have produced, and still keep in place, center and periphery.
4. In North American theology of recent years, Frederick Herzog has been one of the pioneers. Some of his unpublished work on this issue will be made available in Joerg M. Rieger, ed., *Theology from the Belly of the Whale: A Frederick Herzog Reader*, forthcoming from Trinity Press International.

5. Jürgen Moltmann in his contribution to this volume reminds us that political theology did not aim at "politicizing" theology and the churches but at "christianizing" their political existence.

6. Cf. William Wolman, Anne Colamosca, *The Judas Economy: The Triumph of Capital and the Betrayal of Work* (Reading, Mass.: Addison-Wesley, 1997), 4: "Never before has so much Wall Street expertise been handed out to so many so fast."

7. Jeanette Rodríguez, "Experience as a Resource for Feminist Thought," *Journal of Hispanic and Latino Theology* 1:1 (1993), 71.

8. One of the foremost critics of Latin American liberation theology, Michael Novak, sees the worsening situation in Latin America as proof that liberation theology does not work. Michael Novak, "Liberation Theology—What's Left," *First Things* 14:10 (June/July 1991). But why blame liberation theology for the situation of Latin America? Even in Latin America the market economy has always been incomparably more influential than liberation theology. What unites many of the critics of liberation theology is their belief that the free market will solve everything. See Novak, ibid.; and Edward Lynch, "Beyond Liberation Theology," *Journal of Interdisciplinary Studies* 6:1–2 (1994), 161, who believes that, unlike socialism, capitalism allows that love can permeate economic relationships. At the same time many economists are, of course, no longer so optimistic.

9. The Council of Bishops of the United Methodist Church, *Children and Poverty: An Episcopal Initiative* (Nashville: United Methodist Publishing House, 1996), 2.

10. See the United Nations' *Human Development Report 1996* (New York: Oxford University Press, 1996).

11. Deborah Decker, National Public Radio, November 27, 1997.

12. Wolman and Colamosca, *The Judas Economy,* ix, 9. In the summer of 1996 stock prices retreated when the first real gains for wages after twenty years were announced; ibid., 24.

13. "The market is now God." Ibid., 2.

14. David R. Loy, "The Religion of the Market," *Journal of the American Academy of Religion* 65:2 (Summer 1997), 276.

15. See Fredric Jameson, "The Cultural Logic of Late Capitalism," in *Postmodernism, or the Cultural Logic of Late Capitalism* (Durham, N.C.: Duke University Press, 1991).

16. Jean Baudrillard, *America,* trans. Chris Turner (London, New York: Verso, 1988), 111.

17. In the United States 80 million people, 45 percent of the adult public, do volunteer work. See Robert Wuthnow, *Acts of Compassion: Caring for Others and Helping Ourselves* (Princeton: Princeton University Press, 1991), 5–6.

18. This is the problem of the theological tourist: "Tourism depends on the appeal of the exotic other who is different enough to titillate, while not so different that one's sense of being a 'hardened self' is threatened. The tourist can pop in and out of exotic locations with very little time expended and observe without participation." *Beyond Theological Tourism,* ed. Susan Brooks Thistlethewaite and George F. Cairns (Maryknoll, N.Y.: Orbis, 1994), 12–13. For the notion of two-way street, see Joerg Rieger, "The Means of Grace, John Wesley, and the Theological Dilemma of the Church Today," *Quarterly Review* (Winter 1997–98), 377–93.

19. George E. Tinker, *Missionary Conquest: The Gospel and Native American Cultural Genocide* (Minneapolis: Fortress, 1993), 112.

20. Ibid., 3, 17.

21. *Beyond Theological Tourism,* ed. Thistlethwaite and Cairns, 6 and 12.

22. 1 John 4:20 is well known: "Those who do not love a brother or sister whom they have seen, cannot love God whom they have not seen." See also my book

Remember the Poor: The Challenge to Theology in the Twenty-First Century (Harrisburg: Trinity Press International, 1998).

23. The Council of Bishops, *Children and Poverty,* 7.

24. *Liberation Theologies, Postmodernity, and the Americas,* ed. David Batstone, Eduardo Mendieta, Lois Ann Lorentzen, Dwight N. Hopkins (London, New York: Routledge, 1997), 4.

25. See Henry Steele Commager, *The Empire of Reason: How Europe Imagined and America Realized the Enlightenment* (New York: Oxford University Press, 1982). As the title indicates, Commager argues that the Enlightenment was much more powerful in the U.S. than in Europe since it did not have to face the resistance of older structures.

26. Sandra Harding, "The Instability of the Analytical Categories of Feminist Theory," *Signs* 11:4 (1986), 649.

27. Roxanne A. Dunbar, "Bloody Footprints: Reflections on Growing Up Poor White," in *White Trash: Race and Class in America,* ed. Matt Wray and Annalee Newitz (New York and London: Routledge, 1997), 77. Dunbar laments that many critical voices are still dampened by various ideas, including the "religion of 'Americanism,'" referring to the American dream that anyone can make it, and to Manifest Destiny, the belief in the sacred origin and divine purpose of the United States.

28. See Dietrich Bonhoeffer's report as exchange student, "Bericht über den Studienaufenthalt im Union Theological Seminary zu New York 1930/31," in *Gesammelte Schriften* (Munich: Kaiser, 1958), 1: 96–97. Cf. also Bonhoeffer, "Protestantismus ohne Reformation," in ibid., 349.

29. Frederick Herzog, "Reformation Today," *The Christian Century* 99:33 (October 1982), 1079. In *"Praxis Passionis Divini," Evangelische Theologie* 44:6 (November/December 1984), 563–75, Herzog brings together what he sees as the "reformation tradition" and the "liberation tradition." An English translation of this essay is forthcoming in *Theology from the Belly of the Whale: A Frederick Herzog Reader,* ed. Joerg Rieger.

30. Sociologist Rhys H. Williams reminds us that the culture-wars idea "is not the only game in town." Rhys H. Williams, "Is America in a Culture War? Yes—No—Sort of," *The Christian Century* 114:32 (November 12, 1997), 1043. It not only neglects other differences, such as class (and we must add race and gender), it also fails to pay attention to other forms in which people become involved in the life of society.

2. On Being a Traitor

1. Paulo Freire, *Pedagogy of the Oppressed* (New York: Seabury Press, 1994), 19.

2. Nelle Morton, "The Rising Woman Consciousness in a Male Language Structure," *Andover Newton Quarterly* 12 (March 1972): 177–90.

3. See Ernesto Cardenal, *The Gospel in Solentiname* (Maryknoll, N.Y.: Orbis, 1982).

4. Juan Luis Segundo, *Liberation of Theology* (Maryknoll, N.Y.: Orbis, 1976).

5. See Susan Brooks Thistlethwaite, "Every Two Minutes: Battered Women and the Bible," in *Feminist Interpretation of the Bible,* ed. Letty Russell (Philadelphia: Westminster, 1986); and also Elisabeth Schüssler Fiorenza, *Bread Not Stone: The Challenge of Feminist Biblical Interpretation* (Boston: Beacon Press, 1984).

6. Cited in Judith Herman, *Trauma and Recovery* (New York: Basic Books, 1992), 209.

7. Frederick Herzog, *Justice Church: The New Function of the Church in North American Christianity* (Maryknoll, N.Y.: Orbis, 1980), 57.

8. Ibid., 66, citing Friedrich Schleiermacher, *The Christian Faith* (Edinburgh: T & T. Clark, 1928), 565.

9. Herzog, *Justice Church*, 67.

10. Certainly, not all psychological theory falls into this category, as the work of Judith Herman shows. An exception to theological imparting of psychological paradigms would be H. Richard Niebuhr, a prominent Protestant liberal, who used sociology effectively in doing historical analysis. Niebuhr was identifying racism, sexism, and classism as epidemic in American religion long before black or feminist theology was created. See *The Social Sources of Denominationalism* (New York: H. Holt, 1929) as an example.

11. Linda Mercadante, *Victims and Sinners: Spiritual Roots of Addiction and Recovery* (Louisville, Ky.: Westminster John Knox, 1996), 109.

12. Rita Nakashima Brock and Susan Brooks Thistlethwaite, *Casting Stones: Prostitution and Liberation in Asia and the United States* (Minneapolis, Minn.: Fortress, 1996).

13. Mary Potter Engel, "Evil, Sin, and the Violation of the Vulnerable," in eds., *Lift Every Voice: Constructing Christian Theologies from the Underside,* ed. Susan Brooks Thistlethwaite and Mary Potter Engel, 2d ed. (Maryknoll, N.Y.: Orbis, 1998), 155.

14. "State of the World's Children" (UNICEF, 1995).

15. Marian Wright Edelman, "Cease Fire! Stopping the Gun War against Children in the United States," *Chicago Theological Seminary Register* (Winter, 1995).

16. "New York Churches Fight Mayor on 'Workfare,'" *United Church News* (September 1997), 5.

17. "The German Ideology," in Karl Marx and Friedrich Engels, *Collected Works* (New York: International Publishers, 1975–1992), 5:38.

18. Karl Marx, "Comments on James Mill, 'Éléments d'économie politique,'" in *Collected Works* 3:227–28.

19. Thanh-dam Truong, *Sex, Money and Morality: Prostitution and Tourism in Southeast Asia* (Atlantic Highlands, N.J.: Zed Books, 1990).

20. Christine Di Stefano, "Dilemmas of Difference," *Feminism/Postmodernism*, ed. Linda Nicholson (London, New York: Routledge, 1990), 75.

21. Nancy Hartsock, "Foucault on Power: A Theory for Women?" *Feminism/Postmodernism,* ed. Nicholson, 160.

22. Ibid., 163.

23. Ibid., 164.

3. Liberation Theology and the Global Economy

1. Herzog was consistently supportive of my efforts, even asking me to write for a German magazine, translating this, and arranging for publication in order to introduce certain of my ideas into the German discussion. John B. Cobb, Jr., "Katastrophale Wirtschaft: Die weltweiten Folgen des Oekonomismus," *Evangelische Kommentare* (March 1994), 168–70.

2. See José Míguez Bonino, *Christians and Marxists: The Mutual Challenge to Revolution* (Grand Rapids, Mich.: William B. Eerdmans, 1976).

3. See William M. Alexander, "A Sustainable Development Process: Kerala," *International Journal of Sustainable Development* (May 1992), 52–58.

4. See Clifford Cobb, Ted Halsted, and Jonathan Rowe, "If the GDP Is Up, Why Is America Down?" *The Atlantic Monthly* (October 1995), 59–78.

4. Economy and the Future of Liberation Theology

1. By "the poor" I mean here all human and natural creatures who suffer in the various dimensions of oppression: economic, political, cultural, natural, and personal. By "the poor" (*ptochoi* and *ochlos*) the gospels usually mean those who suffer in *all* of these dimensions.

2. The distinction I intend between "economy" and "economics" should become clear below.

3. This is clear in Gustavo Gutiérrez's Introduction to the fifteenth-anniversary edition of his *A Theology of Liberation: History, Politics, and Salvation* (Maryknoll, N.Y.: Orbis, 1988), xvii–xlvi.

4. In North America, Frederick Herzog has been the only white, male theologian to develop a thoroughgoing liberation theology. Among North Americans who "import" liberation theologies from Latin America, Africa, Asia, Black Theology, Feminist Theology, or Native American Theology, the tendency is to stir liberation into a warmed-over liberal soup. Not so Herzog. He wanted to understand liberation theology as dogmatics, the new dogmatics necessary for the life of the North American church. Herzog was through and through what the tradition has called in the best sense a dogmatician. According to Herzog the primary question of the first five centuries of Christian doctrine was the closeness of Jesus to God. In the Reformation era it was God's closeness to the human being. "Today the concern is God's closeness to history in the struggle for *justice*. Thus the traditions today are being examined for their *justice* power. Accountable teaching in the church develops as God's justice struggle is being examined. God-walk compels us to analyze, for example, how we relate to politics and economics. Are we using our commitment to Christ merely to legitimate our life politically and economically? Or does Christ open a way for critical spirituality?" Frederick Herzog, *God-Walk: Liberation Shaping Dogmatics* (Maryknoll, N.Y.: Orbis, 1988), 46. See M. Douglas Meeks, "Dogmatics as Discipleship: The Theological Journey of Frederick Herzog," in *Theology and Corporate Conscience: Essays in Honor of Frederick Herzog*, ed. Jürgen Moltmann and M. Douglas Meeks (forthcoming).

5. See M. Douglas Meeks, *God the Economist: The Doctrine of God and Political Economy* (Minneapolis: Fortress, 1989).

6. Jonathan J. Bonk, *Mission and Money: Affluence as a Western Missionary Problem* (Maryknoll, N.Y.: Orbis, 1991).

7. R. Laurence Moore, *Selling God: American Religion in the Marketplace of Culture* (New York: Oxford University Press, 1994).

8. Denominational leaders see signs of the collapse "in the massive losses suffered by mainstream Protestantism; the alienation of members and congregations from national leadership; resultant diversion of resources away from the denominational coffers into local and regional projects; the growing division within denominations between liberals and evangelicals (and the persisting division between white and black); the emergence of quasi-independent caucuses and struggle-groups, each bent on pressing its agenda and capturing power; and the muting of mainstream Protestant denominations' public voice and/or its eclipse in American society by evangelical and non-Protestant voices." Russell E. Richey, "Denominations and Denominationalism: An American Morphology," in *Reimagining Denominationalism: Interpretive Essays*, ed. by Robert Bruce Mullin and Russell E. Richey (New York: Oxford University Press, 1994), 74. See also Wade Clark Roof and William McKinney, *American Mainline Religion* (New Brunswick, N.J.: Rutgers University Press, 1987); Robert Wuthnow, *The Struggle for America's Soul* (Grand Rapids: Eerdmans, 1989); *idem, The Restructuring of American Religion* (Princeton: Princeton University Press, 1988); Mark A. Noll, *Religion and American Politics: From the Colonial Period to the 1980s* (New

York: Oxford University Press, 1990); Nathan O. Hatch, *The Democratization of American Christianity* (New Haven: Yale University Press, 1989).

9. Theology in the shadow of the Enlightenment considered the modern paradigm shifts in knowledge to be the preeminent problem of the gospel. Postmodern thinking changed the focus to power, or knowledge expressed in power. Deconstructing structures to see their hidden imperatives, critical theory holds that the logics of power and knowledge are logics of violence and control and thereby elucidates the problems of subjugation and dehumanization. Its success is that almost all spheres of scholarship, including theological scholarship, deal with critical theory. Its failure is its impotence to change the trends of the deformation of society and the tyrannizing of nature it so fulsomely describes.

10. Karl Polanyi, *The Great Transformation* (Boston: Beacon, 1957).

11. For the following see Lester C. Thurow, *The Future of Capitalism* (New York: William Morrow, 1996), 242–78.

12. Ibid., 243. Even if there could be an initial equal distribution of goods and opportunities, workers, for many reasons, do not earn the same. With alacrity the market converts equalities into inequalities.

13. Ibid., 253.

14. Ibid., 246.

15. Ibid., 253.

16. See Edward J. Blakely and Mary Gail Snyder, *Fortress America: Gated Communities in the United States* (Washington, D.C.: Brookings Institution Press/Lincoln Institute, 1997), and Richard Moe and Carter Wilkie, *Changing Places: Rebuilding Community and the Age of Sprawl* (New York: Henry Holt, 1997). It is estimated that there are thirty thousand communities where individuals separate themselves from the outside world. These people purchase the services of private police and thus do not want to pay taxes for public security. As a result, twice as much is spent on private police forces as public police forces.

17. See, for example, Robert Bellah et al., *Habits of the Heart: Individualism and Commitment in American Life* (New York: Harper & Row, 1985); and *idem, The Good Society* (New York: Alfred A. Knopf, 1991); John Kenneth Galbraith, *The Culture of Contentment* (New York: Houghton Mifflin, 1992); Christopher Lasch, *The True and Only Heaven: Progress and Its Critics* (New York: W. W. Norton, 1991).

18. See Steve Tipton's chapter, "The Public Church," in Bellah et al., *The Good Society*, 179–219.

19. John Milbank, *Theology and Social Theory: Beyond Secular Reason* (Oxford: Blackwell, 1990).

20. Mark C. Taylor and Esa Saainen, *Imagologies: Media Philosophy* (New York: Routledge, 1994).

21. Meeks, *God the Economist*, 17–19, 170–77.

22. Peter L. Danner, "Personalism and the Problem of Scarcity," *The Forum for Social Economics* 25/1 (Fall 1995), 21–32.

23. For the following see M. Douglas Meeks, "Comment," *The Forum for Social Economics* 25/1 (Fall 1995), 33–36.

24. Danner, "Personalism and the Problem of Scarcity," 30.

25. Ibid.

26. Karl Polanyi, *The Livelihood of Man*, ed. Harry W. Pearson (New York: Academic Press, 1977), 25.

27. Ibid., 27.

28. "Praise is the primary form of the communication of the gospel, the sheer enjoyment and appreciation of it before God 'even when there is no point at all.' All other communication is an overflow of this, the spread of its scent, affirming in appropriate ways, in various situations, the content and delight of praising

God." Daniel W. Hardy and David F. Ford, *Praising and Knowing God* (Phila-delphia: Westminster, 1985), 149. See the comments of Hardy and Ford on the relation of praise and mission, 148–52.

29. Hans Urs von Balthasar, *The Glory of the Lord: A Theological Aesthetics*, vol. 1: *Seeing the Form*, trans. Erasmo Leiva-Merikakis (New York: Crossroad, 1982). See also recent studies of the Psalms: Claus Westermann, *Praise and Lament in the Psalms* (Atlanta: John Knox, 1981); Walter Brueggemann, *The Psalms and the Life of Faith*, ed. Patrick D. Miller (Minneapolis: Fortress, 1995); Patrick D. Miller, *They Cried to the Lord: The Form and Theology of Biblical Prayer* (Minneapolis: Fortress, 1995).

30. See Christopher Morse's helpful view of "testing the spirits" as "faithful disbelief" in *Not Every Spirit: A Dogmatics of Christian Disbelief* (Valley Forge, Pa.: Trinity Press International, 1994).

31. M. Douglas Meeks, "The Future of Theology in a Commodity Society," in *The Future of Theology: Essays in Honor of Jürgen Moltmann*, ed. Miroslav Volf et al. (Grand Rapids: Eerdmans, 1996), 261–66.

32. See Frederick Herzog's creative presentation of the eucharist as the "jus-tice meal" in *God-Walk*, 130–41 and passim.

33. See M. Douglas Meeks, "Trinity, Community and Power," in *Trinity, Community and Power: Mapping Trajectories in Wesleyan Theology*, ed. M. Douglas Meeks, forthcoming. John Milbank, "Can a Gift Be Given? Prolegomena to a Future Trinitarian Metaphysic," *Modern Theology* 11/1 (January 1995), 119–61.

34. Meeks, *God the Economist*, 179.

5. Political Theology and Theology of Liberation

A German version of this essay has been published in Jürgen Moltmann, *Gott im Projekt der modernen Welt: Beiträge zur öffentlichen Relevanz der Theologie* (Gütersloh: Gütersloher Verlag, 1997), 51–72.

1. *Diskussion zur "Theologie der Revolution,"* ed. E. Feil and R. Weth (Munich and Mainz: Chr. Kaiser, 1969); C. Torres, "Revolution: Christian Imperative," in *Revolutionary Priest: The Complete Writings and Messages of Camilo Torres*, ed. John Gerassi (London: Jonathan Cape, 1971), 261–90.

2. G. Gutiérrez, *Theology of Liberation: History, Politics, and Salvation* (New York: Orbis, 1973/1988).

3. J. B. Metz, *Theology of the World* (London: Burns and Oates; New York: Herder and Herder, 1969); *Diskussion zur "politischen Theologie"* (Munich and Mainz: Grünewald, 1969) ed. H. Peukert. J. B. Metz, J. Moltmann, and W. Oelmüller, *Kirche im Prozess der Aufklärung* (Munich: Mainz, 1970); D. Sölle, *Political Theology* (Philadelphia: Fortress, 1974); J. M. Lochman, *Perspektiven politischer Theologie* (Zurich: Theologischer Verlag, 1971); J. Moltmann, *Perspektiven der Theologie: Gesammelte Aufsätze* (Munich: Chr. Kaiser, 1968); J. Moltmann, *Politische Theologie—Politische Ethik: Gesammelte Aufsätze* (Munich and Mainz: Grünewald, 1984). For a good introduction, see S. Wiedenhofer, *Politische Theologie* (Stuttgart: Kohlhammer, 1976); I. Ellacuría, *Teología polít-ica* (San Salvador: Ediciones del Secretariado Social Interdiocesano, 1973).

4. E. Kogon and J. B. Metz et al., *Gott nach Auschwitz: Dimensionen des Massenmords am jüdischen Volk* (Freiburg: Herder, 1979).

5. *Schöpfertum und Freiheit in einer humanen Gesellschaft*, ed. E. Kellner, Marienbader Protokolle (Vienna: Europa Verlag, 1969).

6. R. Garaudy, J. B. Metz, and K. Rahner, *Der Dialog* (Hamburg: Rowohlt, 1966).

7. E. Bloch, *The Principle of Hope* (Cambridge: MIT Press, 1986). On Bloch's influence in the 1960s see: *Ernst Bloch zu Ehren: Beiträge zu seinem Werk—Festschrift zum 80. Geburtstag,* ed. S. Unseld (Frankfurt: Suhrkamp, 1965).

8. H. Gollwitzer, *Werkausgabe* (Munich: Chr. Kaiser, 1988).

9. Hans-Joachim Kraus (moderator), *Das Bekenntnis zu Jesus Christus und die Friedensverantwortung der Kirche: Eine Erklärung des Moderamens des Reformierten Bundes* (Gütersloh: G. Mohn, 1982).

10. B. Klappert and U. Weidner, eds., *Schritte zum Frieden: Theologische Texte zu Frieden und Abrüstung* (Wuppertal: Aussaat, 1983).

11. J. Moltmann, ed., *Friedenstheologie—Befreiungstheologie* (Munich: Chr. Kaiser, 1988).

12. G. Altner, ed., *Ökologische Theologie* (Stuttgart: Kreuz, 1989).

13. J.M. Lochman and J. Moltmann, eds., *Gottes Recht und die Menschenrechte,* Studien und Empfehlungen des Reformierten Weltbundes (Neukirchen: Neukirchener Verlag, 1977); *Rights of Future Generations—Rights of Nature: Proposal for Enlarging the Universal Declaration of Human Rights,* ed. L. Vischer, Studies from the World Alliance of Reformed Churches (Geneva: World Alliance of Reformed Churches, 1990), 19.

14. E. Moltmann Wendel, *Menschenrechte für die Frau* (Munich: Gruenewald, 1994); D. Williams, *Sisters in the Wilderness: The Challenge of Womanist God-Talk* (New York: Orbis, 1994); A. M. Isasi-Díaz, *Mujerista Theology* (Maryknoll, N.Y.: Orbis, 1996).

15. I refer in the following to the great compendium *Mysterium Liberationis: Fundamental Concepts of Liberation Theology,* ed. I. Ellacuria and Jon Sobrino (Maryknoll: Orbis, 1993).

16. Beginnings are documented in: *Teología India: Primer encuentro taller latinoamericano* (Mexico City: Abya-Yala, 1992); *El rostro indio de Dios,* ed. M. M. Marzal (Lima: Pontificia Universidad Católica del Perú, 1991).

17. L. Boff, *Von der Würde der Erde: Ökologie—Politik—Mystik* (Düsseldorf: Patmos, 1994).

18. E. Cardenal, *Cosmic Canticle* (Willimantic, Conn.: Curbstone Press, 1993).

19. *Mysterium Liberationis,* ed. Ellacuría and Sobrino, German edition, vol. 1, 499.

20. *Publik Forum* (July 17, 1992), 15f.

21. H.-P. Martin and H. Schumann, *Die Globalisierungsfalle: Der Angriff auf Demokratie und Wohlstand* (Hamburg: Rowohlt, 1996).

22. H. Noormann, *Armut in Deutschland: Christen vor der neuen sozialen Frage* (Stuttgart: Calwer Verlag, 1991); E. U. Huster, *Armut in Europa* (Opladen: Leske and Budrich, 1996).

6. Black Consciousness

1. A small group of white theologians welcomed the advent of black theology in the late 1960s and were not afraid to acknowledge that blackness as a symbol of oppression and liberation was a much-needed corrective to the theology and praxis of the mainstream churches of North America. Frederick Herzog was possibly the first to participate in that group. His *tour de force* was a provocative exposition of the Fourth Gospel entitled *Liberation Theology: Liberation in Light of the Fourth Gospel* (New York: Seabury Press, 1972), a book that was a welcome surprise to those who were trying to create a black liberation theology, but a shock to most of his white colleagues.

2. Unfortunately, most of us were too involved in the movement to empower the black community to give Herzog's contribution the attention it deserved. I

recall, however, that we were all grateful to this rather aberrant white professor in—of all places, North Carolina! where court-ordered desegregation was being bitterly fought in Charlotte and Wilmington—who could bring the two words "black" and "theology" together without choking in the process. James Cone observed that Herzog was the only white theologian he knew who was prepared to reorder the priorities of the new political theology in the light of black oppression. "Whatever else may be said about Herzog's *Liberation Theology*," Cone wrote, "it is concrete evidence that white theologians do not have to remain enclosed in their little white boxes." James H. Cone, *God of the Oppressed* (New York: Seabury Press, 1975), 50.

3. C. Eric Lincoln, *The Black Church since Frazier* (New York: Schocken Books, 1974), 106–107.

4. For a discussion of ancient rabbinical interpretations of blackness see Edith R. Sanders, "The Hamitic Hypothesis," *Journal of African History*, 10 (1969), 521–32; Robert Graves and Raphael Patai, *Hebrew Myths: The Book of Genesis* (New York: Greenwich House, 1983); and Charles B. Copher, *Black Biblical Studies: An Anthology of Charles B. Copher* (Chicago: Black Light Fellowship, 1993), 102–104. A broader examination of color symbolism and implications for anti-black attitudes is found in the classical essay by Roger Bastide, "Color, Racism, and Christianity," in John Hope Franklin, *Color and Race* (Boston: Houghton Mifflin Co., 1968), 34–49.

5. Although the matter continues to be in dispute among biblical scholars, for centuries Noah's curse has been associated with the people of Africa and those of African descent by reference to the descendants of Ham as enumerated in Genesis 10:6–14.

6. Victor Anderson, *Beyond Ontological Blackness: An Essay on African American Religious and Cultural Criticism* (New York: Continuum, 1995).

7. Gabriel M. Setiloane, "I Am an African," in *Mission Trends, No. 3: Third World Theologies*, ed. Gerald H. Anderson and Thomas F. Stransky, C.S.P. (New York: Paulist Press and Wm. B. Eerdmans Publishing Co., 1976), 130–31.

8. Frederick Herzog, *Justice Church: The New Function of the Church in North American Christianity* (Maryknoll: Orbis, 1980), 146.

7. Liberation Theology and the Future of the Poor

1. Cf. G. Gutiérrez, "Teología: una función eclesial," *Páginas* 130 (Dec. 1994), 10–17; and *Münchener Theologische Zeitschrift* 47:2 (1996), 162–71.

2. Cf. F. Herzog, *God-Walk: Liberation Shaping Dogmatics* (New York: Orbis, 1988).

3. Contextual theologies are sometimes referred to as a special type of understanding of faith. It depends on the meaning, because in a manner of speaking all of theology is contextual, without putting into question what is permanent in that effort.

4. Speech delivered on September 11, 1962.

5. John Paul II has referred to this numerous times. For example, remembering that Jesus came to evangelize the poor (in reference to Matt. 11: 5 and Luke 7: 22), the question arises, "Why not underscore more decidedly the preferential option of the church for the poor and the marginalized?"

6. This point is clearly stated by J. Dupont, *Les Béatitudes*, vol. 3 (Paris: Gabalda, 1964–1969). On the same issue see J. Schlosser, *Le Règne de Dieu dans les dits de Jésus* (Paris: Gabalda, 1980).

7. In this perspective of change in relation to the parable of the Good Samaritan we cited E. Levinas in G. Gutiérrez, *A Theology of Liberation: History,*

Politics and Salvation, trans. Sister Caridad Inda and John Eagleson (Maryknoll: Orbis, 1973 and 1988), 202, n.41 and 230, n.41.

8. E. Levinas, *De Dieu qui vient à l'idee* (Paris: Vrin, 1982), 145.

9. J. C. Scannone has shown the richness of this point of view in philosophy; cf. "La irrupción del pobre y la pregunta filosófica en América Latina" in *Irrupción del pobre y quehacer filosófico* (Buenos Aires: Bonum, 1993), 123–40.

10. For more on the subject of national economies and the global economy, see Robert B. Reich, *The Work of Nations* (New York: Vintage Books, 1992).

11. There has been discussion of a third revolutionary wave in the history of humanity. This theme is popularized by the works of A. and H. Tofler. Cf. Also T. Sakaiya, *Historia del futuro: la sociedad del conocimiento* (Santiago de Chile: Editorial Andres Bello, 1994). These works carry an optimistic tone but are less attentive perhaps to the actual reversal of this revolution of knowledge for the poorest sectors of the world's population.

12. Despite its achievements in the 1960s and 1970s, the theory of dependency (in reality, more an intuition than a systematic theory) present within the margins of liberation theology in the corresponding chapter of the knowledge of the socioeconomic reality, is today an inadequate tool to explain newer developments, new forms of dependency, and enormous complexity of the current state of affairs. Cf. the study by C. Kay, *Latin American Theories of Development and Underdevelopment* (London and New York: Routledge, 1989). The appropriate approach of a science that seeks to be rigorous, including of dangerous grounds like the social arena, is to be open to new hypothesis and possibilities.

13. The text continues with very harsh terms: the love of money is "one of these inclinations and semi-pathological (conditions) that are placed in the hands of mental disease specialists."

14. "Economic Possibilities for our Grandchildren" in *The Collected Writings: Essays in Persuasion*, vol. 9, 3rd ed., (London: MacMillan, 1972), 329–30, 331. For an ethical and economic critique of economic liberalism, see, among other works, M. Douglas Meeks, *God the Economist: The Doctrine of God and Political Economy* (Minneapolis: Fortress, 1989).

15. It is important to note that in certain Christian and theological circles a favorable view of liberal economy can be found, in particular in the United States, where there is a large bibliographical production. See, for example, M. Novak, *The Spirit of Democratic Capitalism* (New York: Simon and Schuster, 1982).

16. "Inhumana miseria" (Medellín, n.1), "antievangélica pobreza" (Puebla, n.1159), "el más devastador y humillante flagelo que vive América Latina y el Caribe" (Santo Domingo, n.179).

17. *Informe* (1996), 2. In the last thirty years the income per capita of the poorest fifth of the world's population went from 2.3 percent (already far too low) to 1.4 percent. In contrast, the income per capita of the richest fifth grew from 70 percent to 85 percent, "so it doubled the ratio between the proportion corresponding to the richest and to the poorest, from 30:1 to 60:1" (l.c.).

18. We add that the poorest regions of Latin America present the greatest inequality in the distribution of salaries. Cf. *Informe de la comisión latinoamericana y del Caribe sobre el desarrollo social* (1995).

19. *Economic Justice for All* (1986) n.87. Emphasis in original.

20. This criterion brings to mind the second principle of justice by J. Rawls, *Teoría de la justicia*, 2nd ed. (Mexico: FCE, 1996), 68; English translation: *Theory of Justice* (Cambridge, Mass: Belknap Press of Harvard University Press, 1971)— with the variety of consequences for the poor that we have already alluded to.

21. Homily of the mass that was celebrated in the Namao airport (Canada) September 17, 1984, nn.3–4. My emphasis.

22. "Extremely simplifying matters, one can understand the postmodern as the incredulity regarding metanarratives." J. F. Lyotard, *La condition postmoderne* (Paris: Editions de Minuit, 1979), 7; English translation: *The Postmodern Condition: Report on Knowledge* (Minneapolis: University of Minnesota Press, 1984).

23. J. F. Lyotard, *La postmodernidad explicada a los niños* (Barcelona: Gedisa, 1987), 29; English translation: *Postmodernity Explained to Children: Correspondence, 1982–85* (Minneapolis: University of Minnesota Press, 1993).

24. Cf. ibid.

25. *La condition postmoderne*, 7. In this sense Marxism constitutes one of these metanarratives.

26. "Modernity," says G. Vattimo, "ceases to exist when for various reasons the possibility of speaking about history as a unified entity disappears." G. Vattimo, "Posmodernidad ¿una sociedad transparente?" in *En torno a la posmodernidad* (Barcelona: Anthropos, 1990), 10. Vattimo sees the same fundamental move, but with some divergencies from Lyotard: "What is being sought is to consider and to calibrate that which makes up the dissolution of the foundational thought, that is: metaphysics." G. Vattimo,"Posmodernidad y fin de la historia," *Etica de la interpretación* (Barcelona: Paidos, 1991), 28. Inspired by Friedrich Nietzsche and Martin Heidegger, he postulates that which qualifies as "weak thought" and clarifies that this "is not a weak thought, but the weakening or breakdown: the acknowledgment of a line of dissolution within the history of ontology." Cited in T. Oñate, "Introducción," in G. Vattimo, *La sociedad transparente* (Barcelona: Paidos, 1990), 38.

27. Agnes Heller, "Los movimientos culturales," in *Colombia: el despertar de la modernidad,* ed. F. Viviescas and F. Giraldo (Bogota: Foro Nacional de Colombia, 1991).

28. Cf. C. Lash, *The Culture of Narcisism: American Life in an Age of Diminishing Expectations* (New York-London: Norton, 1991).

29. These lines are inspired by what has been said in G. Gutiérrez, *A Theology of Liberation*, 23–24, and *We Drink from Our Own Wells: The Spiritual Journey of a People*, trans. Matthew J. O'Connell (Maryknoll: Orbis, 1984), 91–92.

30. For this reason we speak of three dimensions of integral liberation that are not confused nor juxtaposed: social liberation, personal liberation, and soteriological liberation: liberation from sin, and communion with God and with others.

31. "Subida del Monte Carmelo," in *Vida y Obras de San Juan de la Cruz* (Madrid: BAC, 1950), 558; English translation: *Ascent of Mount Carmel*, 3rd rev. ed. (Garden City, N.Y.: Image Books, 1958).

32. We repeat some points here presented in our article "Relectura de San Juan de la Cruz desde América Latina" in *Actas del Congreso Internacional San Juanista*, vol. 3 (Junta de Castilla y León, 1993), 325–35.

33. For these reasons those who think—and write—that liberation theology has only in these recent years entered into the terrain of spirituality and mysticism, due to the debates going on around it, are familiar with neither the sources nor the breadth of this reflection on faith.

34. In one of his last articles, Frederick Herzog expresses with great sensitivity the interest of theological reflection that comes from the Native American people of North America; cf. "New Birth of Conscience," *Theology Today* 54:3 (January 1997): 477–84, also included in this volume.

35. We can observe in our times a point that becomes clear in the dialogue of humanity's great religions, which is equally important in some cases in Latin America. It concerns Jesus Christ, the Son of God made human, one of us within history, Jewish, son of Mary, belonging to a particular ethnic group. The his-

toricity of Jesus can create problems for religious perspectives that find it difficult to accept elements that they judge as coming out of their cultural traditions.
Nevertheless, the historical character of the Incarnation is a central element of
the Christian faith. It would be necessary to deepen, in all cases, the significance
of the categories of ideas within and outside of our own history.

36. It is interesting to see how the perspective of death and life is taken into
consideration in the economy; cf. the work of Amartya Sen, "La vida y la muerte
como indicadores economicos," *Investigación y Ciencia* (July 1993), 6–13.

37. Cf. J. Moltmann, *The Future of Creation: Collected Essays* (Philadelphia:
Fortress, 1979); R. Coste, *Dieu et l'ecologie* (Paris: Editions de l'Atelier, 1994); and
Ecology and Poverty: Cry of the Earth, Cry of the Poor, ed. L. Boff and V. Elizondo,
(London: SCM Press, Maryknoll, N.Y.: Orbis, 1995).

8. Developing a Common Interest Theology
from the Underside

1. Frederick Herzog, review of Richard Shaull, *The Reformation and
Liberation Theology: Insights for the Challenges of Today,* in *Theology Today* 50/2
(July 1993), 290.

2. The first of my teachers to make me think in new ways about the relationship of theory and praxis was Frederick Herzog. I first encountered him in a
course on nineteenth-century European theology at Duke University. Once someone challenged him on the importance of the work of Ludwig Feuerbach for theology. Was Feuerbach merely a master of suspicion? In response he summarized
one of Feuerbach's concerns in this way: "Don't think as a thinker but as a living
being." Obviously, liberation theology came to this insight not through Feuerbach
but in its encounters with people at the underside of history. For me, however, this
was a completely new insight. In the halls of German theology I had been taught,
implicitly or explicitly, that the goal was to think more as a thinker and less as
a living being.

3. As I have pointed out in the Introduction to this volume, I use the designations First World and Third World warily, because they are not unproblematic.
I will keep them, however, because they remind us of actual relationships of
political and economic power.

4. Volker Küster discusses liberation theology as the latest stage of contextual theology. The special shape of the context does not really matter, the social location of the poor and oppressed is not even mentioned in Küster's list of the six
"essential breakthroughs." See Volker Küster, "Models of Contextual Hermeneutics: Liberation and Feminist Theological Approaches Compared,"
Exchange 23/2 (September 1994), 162.

5. See Rudolf Bultmann, "Is Exegesis without Presuppositions Possible?" in
Rudolf Bultmann, *The New Testament and Mythology and Other Basic Writings,*
ed. and trans. Schubert M. Ogden (Philadelphia: Fortress, 1984), 145–53. Per
Frostin, "The Hermeneutics of the Poor: The Epistemological 'Break' in Third
World Theologies," *Studia Theologia* 39 (1985), 146, notes Rudolf Bultmann's
"monolithic view of the present," according to which the notion of "modern man"
comprises all classes, races, and even the sexes.

6. See Paul Tillich, *Systematic Theology,* vol. 2 (Chicago: University of
Chicago Press, 1957), 28. Those categories are of course borrowed from existen-
tialism, but Tillich was convinced that such analyses are "as old as man's thinking about himself." Cf. *Systematic Theology,* vol. 1 (Chicago: University of
Chicago Press, 1951), 62.

7. Cf. Küster, "Models of Contextual Hermeneutics: Liberation and Feminist Theological Approaches Compared." European theology, Bultmann, and Gerhard von Rad are the models; and the poor are not even mentioned.

8. Edward Lynch, "Beyond Liberation Theology," *Journal of Interdisciplinary Studies* 6/1–2 (1994), 151.

9. Frederick Herzog, "United Methodism in Agony," *Perkins Journal* 28/1 (Fall 1974), 1–10. Reprinted in *Doctrine and Theology in the United Methodist Church*, ed. Thomas A. Langford (Nashville: Kingswood Books, 1991), 26–38.

10. Ibid., 33.

11. See, e.g., Rebecca Chopp's comment that "feminism is not somehow just about women; rather, it casts its voice from the margins over the whole of the social-symbolic order, questioning its rules, terms, procedures, and practices." Rebecca Chopp, *The Power to Speak: Feminism, Language, God* (New York: Crossroad, 1991), 16.

12. Susan Secker, "Women's Experience in Feminist Theology: The 'Problem' or the 'Truth' of Difference," *Journal of Hispanic and Latino Theology* 1/1 (1993), 65.

13. Bultmann, "Is Exegesis without Presuppositions Possible?" 153, n.6: "It goes without saying that the existential relation to history does not have to be raised to consciousness. It may only be spoiled by reflection."

14. Gustavo Gutiérrez, "Church of the Poor," in *Born of the Poor: The Latin American Church since Medellín*, ed. Edward L. Cleary, O.P. (Notre Dame, Ind.: University of Notre Dame Press, 1990), 16.

15. Osmundo Afonso Miranda, "A Partial Preface to North American Liberation Theology," in *Liberation Theology: North American Style*, ed. Deane William Ferm (New York: International Religious Foundation, 1987), 28.

16. Walter Benjamin, "Theses on the Philosophy of History," in *Illuminations: Essays and Reflections* (New York: Schocken Books, 1969), 257.

17. Frederick Herzog, "New Christology: Core of New Ecclesiology?" Review of several books by Latin American liberation theologians (L. Boff, G. Cook, G. Gutiérrez, L. Segundo, J. Sobrino) *Religious Studies Review* 14 (July 1988), 216.

18. Among the few exceptions is the work of Toni Morrison, who has made important contributions to understanding this problem. See, for instance, her book *Playing in the Dark: Whiteness and the Literary Imagination* (New York: Vintage Books, 1993).

19. See, e.g., the work of Ada María Isasi-Díaz for *mujerista* theology and the work of Delores Williams for womanist theology. In her book *Sisters in the Wilderness* (Maryknoll, N.Y.: Orbis Books, 1993), 185 ff., Williams discusses the scope of patriarchy from the perspective of black women, which includes class and race issues.

20. Sheila Greeve Davaney invites theology to pay attention not only to the texts and doctrines of the church but to "more ordinary sites of religious meaning including, especially, those of the socially and culturally marginalized." See Sheila Greeve Davaney, "Conclusion: Changing Conversations: Impetuses and Implications," in *Changing Conversations: Religious Reflection and Cultural Analysis*, ed. Dwight N. Hopkins and Sheila Greeve Davaney (New York, London: Routledge, 1996), 255.

21. Mary McClintock Fulkerson, *Changing the Subject: Women's Discourses and Feminist Theology* (Minneapolis: Fortress, 1994), 113.

22. Some economists have realized this before most theologians. Cf. William Wolman and Anne Colamosca, *The Judas Economy: The Triumph of Capital and the Betrayal of Work* (Reading, Mass.: Addison-Wesley, 1997), 2: "The market is now God."

23. Herzog is most likely the first North American liberation theologian to sense already in the 1970s that "Adam Smith's image of man as economic man

still dominates our political and economic relationships, in fact, our entire existence." Cf. Frederick Herzog, "The Political Gospel," *The Christian Century* 87/46 (November 1, 1970), 1381.

24. In much of postmodern thought pluralism exists for its own sake since the postmodern emphasis on difference fails to take into account social contradictions. See Teresa L. Ebert, "The 'Difference' of Postmodern Feminism," *College English* 53/8 (December 1991), 899. I agree with Ebert that differences are not free-floating but related to social contradictions. For this reason, the "other" inscribed within the system needs to be taken more seriously.

25. This is one of the points emphasized strongly in Gustavo Gutiérrez, *We Drink from Our Own Wells: The Spiritual Journey of a People*, foreword by Henri Nouwen, trans. Matthew J. O'Connell (Maryknoll, N.Y.: Orbis, 1984).

26. These are the main questions of Gustavo Gutiérrez, *The God of Life*, trans. Matthew J. O'Connell (Maryknoll, N.Y.: Orbis, 1991); and Gustavo Gutiérrez, *On Job: God-Talk and the Suffering of the Innocent*, trans. Matthew J. O'Connell (Maryknoll, N.Y.: Orbis, 1987).

27. Herzog started to use this term long before Ray S. Anderson, who in his book *Ministry on the Fireline: A Practical Theology for an Empowered Church* (Downers Grove, Ill.: InterVarsity Press, 1993), 212–13, n.2, claims that he invented the term in 1984. See Frederick Herzog, "Doing Liberation Theology in the South," *National Institute for Campus Ministries: Southern Regional Newsletter* 1:2 (January 1976), 7; and Herzog, *Justice Church: The New Function of the Church in North American Christianity* (Maryknoll, N.Y.: Orbis, 1980), 50.

28. Frederick Herzog, "Athens, Berlin, and Lima," *Theology Today* 51/2 (July 1994), 274.

29. Cf. Joerg Rieger, *Remember the Poor: The Challenge to Theology in the Twenty-First Century* (Harrisburg, Pa.: Trinity Press International, 1998).

30. In the first Theology in the Americas Conference in 1975 this point met with the resistance of others, most notably from Hugo Assmann. Reported by Alfred T. Hennelly "Who Does Theology in the Americas?" *America* (September 20, 1975), 139. Cf. also Frederick Herzog, "Introduction: On Liberating Liberation Theology," Introduction to Hugo Assmann, *Theology for a Nomad Church* (Maryknoll, N.Y.: Orbis, 1976), 16.

31. Frederick Herzog, "New Birth of Conscience," *Theology Today* 53/4 (January 1997), 481. This article is reprinted in this volume.

32. Antonio Gramsci, *Selection from the Prison Notebooks,* ed. and trans. Quintin Hoare and Geoffrey Nowell Smith (New York: International Publishers, 1971), 7.

33. This quotation was brought to my attention by an Australian colleague, Deidre Palmer. It is also referred to in Jim Wallis, *The Soul of Politics: A Practical and Prophetic Vision for Change*, foreword by Garry Wills, preface by Cornel West (New York and Maryknoll, N.Y.: New Press and Orbis, 1994), 152.

34. According to the estimate of historians. Cf. Frederick Herzog, "New Birth of Conscience," 479.

35. Frederick Herzog, "*Tradición Común* Shaping Christian Theology: Mutualization in Theological Education," *Working Paper Series* 12 (April 1994), Duke-UNC Program in Latin American Studies, 6–7, also included in *Theology from the Belly of the Whale: A Frederick Herzog Reader*, ed. Joerg Rieger, forthcoming from Trinity Press International. This paper reports on the preliminary results of an effort to initiate "research on the shared memories and interests as well as the complicities of North and South in order to arrive at a 'mutualization' of theological education." (Cf. abstract.)

36. Gustavo Gutiérrez, *A Theology of Liberation: History, Politics, and Salvation*, trans. Sister Caridad Inda and John Eagleson, revised 15th anniver-

sary edition with a new introduction by the author (Maryknoll, N.Y.: Orbis, 1988), xxxvi, sees the importance of international theological dialogues "not in the coming together of theologians, but in the communication established among Christian communities and their respective historical, social, and cultural contexts, for these communities are the real subjects who are actively engaged in these discourses of faith." Cf. also Frederick Herzog, "Kirchengemeinschaft im Schmelztiegel—Anfang einer neuen Ökumene?" in *Kirchengemeinschaft im Schmelztiegel*, ed. Frederick Herzog and Reinhard Groscurth (Neukirchen Vluyn: Neukirchener Verlag, 1989), 28–70.

37. Frederick Herzog, "Wenn Supermacht zum Götzen wird," *Evangelische Kommentare* 8/8 (August 1975), 458 (translation mine).

9. New Birth of Conscience

The late Frederick Herzog, Professor of Systematic Theology at Duke University and author of numerous books, including *God-Walk: Shaping Dogmatics* (1988), completed this article shortly before his death on October 9, 1995. It first appeared in *Theology Today* 53/4 (January 1997), 477–84, reprinted by permission.

1. George E. Tinker, *Missionary Conquest: The Gospel and Native American Cultural Genocide* (Minneapolis: Fortress, 1993), viii–ix.

2. William C. Placher, "Why Bother with Theology?" *The Christian Century* 111 (February 2–9, 1994), 104–108.

3. *The Living Lincoln*, ed. Paul M. Angle and Earl Schenck Miers (New Brunswick: Rutgers University Press, 1955), 522.

4. Walter J. Hollenweger, "Theologie tanzen: Warum wir eine 'narrative Exegese' brauchen," *Evangelische Kommentare* 7 (1995), 403 (my translation).

5. Ibid.

6. Quoted in David E. Stannard, *American Holocaust: The Conquest of the New World* (New York: Oxford University Press, 1992), 127.

7. Quoted in ibid., 126.

8. Ibid., 261–68.

9. Sidney G. Hall III, *Christian Anti-Semitism and Paul's Theology* (Minneapolis: Fortress, 1993), 19.

10. Ibid., 19–20.

11. Ibid., 139–40.

12. Ibid., 138–39.

13. Dietrich Bonhoeffer, *Letters and Papers from Prison*, enlarged ed. (New York: Macmillan, 1972), 17; quoted in Hall, *Christian Anti-Semitism*, 140.

14. Terrence W. Tilley, et al., *Postmodern Theologies: The Challenge of Religious Diversity* (Maryknoll, N.Y.: Orbis, 1995).

15. *Theology without Foundations: Religious Practice and the Future of Theological Truth,* ed. Stanley Hauerwas, Nancey Murphy, and Mark Nation, (Nashville: Abingdon, 1994).

16. Vincent van Gogh, *Letters to Emile Bernard* (New York, 1938), 44.

17. Vine Deloria Jr., in *American Studies Newsletter* (January, 1995).

18. Quoted in Tilley, *Postmodern Theologies*, 70.

19. Stanley Hauerwas, "Remembering as a Moral Task: The Challenge of the Holocaust," in *Against the Nations: War and Survival in a Liberal Society* (Notre Dame: University of Notre Dame Press, 1992), 61–90.

20. Irving Greenberg, "Cloud of Smoke, Pillar of Fire: Judaism, Christianity, and Modernity after the Holocaust," in *Auschwitz: Beginning of a New Era? Reflections on the Holocaust*, ed. Eva Fleischner (New York: KTAV, 1977), 23; quoted in Hall, *Christian Anti-Semitism*, v.

Index